# MORE TALES OF A ROCK STAR'S DAUGHTER

## Nettie Baker

# MORE TALES OF A ROCK STAR'S DAUGHTER

## Nettie Baker

**WP**
**WYMER**
PUBLISHING
Bedford, England

First published in Great Britain in 2019
by Wymer Publishing
Bedford, England
www.wymerpublishing.co.uk
Tel: 01234 326691
Wymer Publishing is a trading name of Wymer (UK) Ltd

**ISBN 978-1-912782-21-5**

Edited by Jerry Bloom.

Typeset by The Andys
Printed and bound in Great Britain by
Clays Ltd, Bungay, Suffolk

A catalogue record for this book is available from the British Library.

Cover design by The Andys.
Cover photos © Nettie Baker.
Back cover photos:
Top row mohicans:  Me, Leda & Pinz all 1986
Top to bottom: Top: Me, Zillah & Sid, (Rubella Ballet) 2018 (pic courtesy of Ealing Club)
Middle: Daughter Zara, John Lydon & me, 100 Club, London, 2018
Bottom: me with Rat Scabies, London, 2013.

# PART TWO 1985-87

DEDICATED TO MY MARVELLOUS CHILD,
ZARA LOUVAINE LEWIS
& REMEMBERING 'BIG' LISA, NIG
& IAN CHAMBERS WITH LOVE.

*Thanks for help with images to Justine Armatage, Paula Ann Mitchell, Lisa Robinson, Sid n Zillah & to all my mates for everything!*

# 'Sound of the Suburbs'

*'In the city centre, you're saturated with information overload, but in Harrow, Ealing, Bromley, Enfield, you're close enough to sample its pleasures first hand, yet far away enough to process the information and put it together in a new way.'*

Jon Savage

# CONTENTS

# PREFACE

To fully understand what's going on here you really do need to read the first volume of *Tales of a Rock Star's Daughter* (Wymer Publishing, 2018) & also the book I ghost-wrote in 2009, *Hellraiser: Ginger Baker*. If you haven't, you may wonder who some of these characters are and how on earth I got to be a punk rocker on the dole in 1985!

But many new characters are introduced here, and as a stand-alone this serves as a pub-based soap opera of troubled young lives set against a grim London backdrop. This is the flip side of the 'greed is good' era of Thatcher's Britain.

A Daily Mail journalist thought I was 'promiscuous' in book one and that was an innocent stroll through the park compared to what I get up to here! Promiscuity is really an anachronism now I hope, with us all being judged equally on our actions and we at this time, were the first to do so. Don't see these tales as harsh, but as uplifting as I do. The search for identity found its conclusion; bonds were forged that still endure and I will stick my neck out and say I 'sort of' really fell in love twice and had my heart broken twice simultaneously (at the end of 1986).

Here is a different planet and time is 'another country', where the wild things were. Looking back once or twice very briefly to meet Jimi Hendrix and forward to Cream's RAH reunion in 2005. See Live Aid from the cheap seats. Rebellion, eviction, squats, gigs, speed, smack, booze and glue aligned to mohicans, chains, tattoos, make-up, love, sex and heart-break. Petty squabbles, betrayals, bloody fights, doomed and dirty youth. This is a love story on many levels and a proof of dreams come true!

# CHAPTER ONE
## 'This Ain't No Party': 1985

Ah, we've now got to the wild excitement of 'Part Two' (See Book One!). I seem to have lived my life a bit backwards where money is concerned because any retrospective of the Eighties, apart from looking at The Miner's Strike, is keen to highlight the twin themes of 'greed' and 'yuppiedom'. Of course the boom and bust cycle was also in play, but we saw no boom at all at my end. Therefore, whilst the majority apparently enjoyed vast amounts of newly acquired wealth and went about quaffing champagne in up market wine bars, my mother, siblings and I hit the financial skids big time. But even though materially bereft, we seemed to find the wherewithal in our psyches to have a good time no matter what life may have seen fit to throw at us and I for one was looking to the community based spirit of the Harrow scene to offer me an alternative to my downers.

Back on New Year's Day 1985 however, I had a few more perilous ledges to negotiate before I finally arrived at the destination I had set my sights on, which was to become fully integrated with the Punks. I had of course completely forgotten all about that ambition as I lay contentedly in Dennis's wiry arms and the embryonic year dawned still and grey. He was supposed to get up early and take his mother and whoever to the airport, but was so busy with me that he missed them and we stayed in bed for a few more hours. Dennis and I finally got up and together we walked up to The Castle for more alcohol. His ex was there and she seemed very pleased that we had got together and was as always, showering me with advice. None of which worked at all because it was her he wanted to be with and he obviously didn't agree with the good old loving the one you're with stuff either.

He then took me to the The Tandoor and bought me a meal (quite an amazing thing in those times) and we went back to The Castle until the grumpy landlord threw Shuggy and I out of the pub for laughing. (Shuggy was a very mad, bad, hilarious, black haired, bearded and scary Scotsman, whom according to rumour, had had something to do with a shooting up in Glasgow. He usually hung about with Legs, an immensely tall, broad and equally awe-inspiring individual with very long brown hair and who sometimes wore a top hat.) Once deposited upon the pavement, we all decided to go off and find somewhere else and in the ensuing confusion of getting lifts here and there from whoever, we must've lost the unsteady Dennis somewhere on the Hill, because he never arrived at The Swan in South Harrow with the rest of us. Now don't say he did it on purpose, because of course now I see it as highly likely, but back then I was truly distraught. In the end, one of my little old admirers gave me a lift home to Grandma's in his three-wheeler and on the way he asked me out. I could have wept.

For the next ten days I flailed about in the depths of despair, although I still managed to chat up some youngsters and be lively when the occasion demanded. I didn't see Dennis at all, but his well-meaning ex kept on with the idea that all would be okay. Perhaps she just wanted him off her case? On Friday 11th January, a very attractive female member of the hippy gang, called Cherie (who drove an ambulance for a living), had a party at her place, high in a tower block in Edgware. We all met up at The Plough and shock, gasp, faint with pleasure, 1812 Overture begins playing in the background; who should be there but Dennis.

At the party, Alison Moyet's 'Invisible' came on and I asked The Menace to dance with me to it, which he did, so I sang the lyrics loudly into his ear. Lots of other bods were dancing attendance but it was they who may as well have been invisible to me. After some time Pikes came up to me and said, 'You'd better go and lie in the hall Nettie.' As that is where Dennis had finally come to rest upon the floor, lying awkwardly prone with his legs blocking the thoroughfare. Consequently, I sat down with my favourite old drunk and at least he couldn't run away. Amazingly, he appeared to be happy to see me and didn't want me to go. Then his minders from the inner sanctum came to rescue him and they thought it would be a good idea for me to join them. I didn't need asking twice. Actually, I think they were glad to have the extra help because it was quite a mammoth task indeed getting him up, into the lift, into the car and out of it again. When we got to his room he just fell into everything, knocking it flying, whilst forcing me to utter the refrain, 'We ain't bothered, they are,' over and over again. His sister Marita asked me if I wanted a lift home. Are you mad? So there we were in bed again, a paralytic Dennis and a drunk but triumphant me. True love eh?

This second attempt at togetherness was slightly more successful than the first, in that it lasted a bit longer. Dennis lived in a shared house with his sister, another girl known as 'Len' and her (very drunken) bloke, Alec. They were a bit of a scary lot to spend a weekend with and the amount they drank surpassed anything that I had so far encountered. The next day we went to a pub called The Narrow Boat, where a couple of gay girls tried to chat me up. I thought they had good taste. We got a cab back, stopping at an Off Licence on the way and I was treated to Dennis singing Chelsea football songs at the top of his voice for the entire journey. We went back to bed.

Then I said I needed to go home and Dennis said, 'Suit yourself,' like a spoiled child until I explained that I just needed to take my pill, get changed and drop the dog off. (In case you're wondering, I always walked and fed the dog whatever the circumstances!) So we got yet another cab to West Harrow and I met them back at some mates of theirs house in Vaughan Road. Another of Dennis's admirers turned up and was surprised to see me there I can tell you. Dennis then proceeded to stumble and fall over everything as usual, his encore being to hurtle through this poor couple's stereo, causing the music to cease directly and those of us who were still conscious to try and make an undignified exit into the street where it was snowing hard.

The bright light of the winter sun reflecting off the snow crashed through the curtains that Sunday morning as alarmingly as dear Dennis himself. As we had eaten hardly anything the day before I was dying of hunger, yet I starved happily and in silence. We got yet another cab down to The Rising Sun in Sudbury where there was a good band on and it continued to snow madly outside; an apt backdrop to such chaotic times.

At closing time, we turned up our collars and shuffled off to a corner store, where we bought some food to cook and walked back to Robin Hood Way. The two girls (helped a bit by me) cooked a magnificent dinner and we chatted cosily in the kitchen, whilst Dennis and Alec played their guitars and sang. We ate, we went to bed, we went to a pub, it carried on snowing; we went to bed. Dennis played the Talking Head's track 'This Ain't No Party' repeatedly and I, fool that I was, thought it meant something but I forgot to pay attention to the bit that says, *'I ain't got time for that now'.*

Monday arrived and the real world came with it, which was probably just as well as far as my health was concerned, because these people must've been superhuman to survive the amount of booze that they consumed. I had to go and sign on and Dennis had to go and pick up a mate whose car wouldn't start. We drew the curtains back and saw that it was snowing again. He kissed me and gave me my bus fare. 'See you later' he said.

Oh no, haven't we been here before? Yes and we will be here again. The prize I thought I'd netted (no pun intended) slipped from my grasp once more. I must stop counting my chickens before they're hatched, but in fact I'd already had them for dinner and done the washing up as well by then. So I stood at a freezing bus stop for an hour, which was time enough to relive each moment and to come to terms with my loss. Three old people stood with me moaning on about everything and I thought, 'Ho hum, this is more like life as I know it.' The bus arrived and I sat upstairs on the scratchy, tartan-patterned wool seat as we made our way slowly along the frozen, white streets towards the dole office.

Snow continued to fall and so inevitably did my spirits. During the days, we all went into sledging overdrive and Harrow Hill was the perfect place for it. My sister Leda and I made a contraption that featured metal runners for extra speed and we had a bad crash when I decided to bail out as a large tree came looming towards us. As a result of this foolhardy decision, I had an enormous black bruise on my leg for ages and Leda banged her head and was convinced she was going to die of delayed concussion and that it was all my fault. Another time, we became entangled with an unfortunate individual who was travelling at a much slower speed in front of us. We urgently gesticulated for him to get out of the way but it was too late and he completed the journey impaled on the front of our sledge with a panic stricken look upon his face. Some of the madder hippies were intent on snowboarding perilously down the graveyard paths, thankfully before they'd had a skinful.

On the Thursday, we caught the 183 bus up to the Plough in sub zero temperatures, where Dennis's ex continued to reassure me that all was hunky dory between us. She couldn't have been more wrong. The next day I was walking through Harrow when I bumped into a woman I recognised from that house in Vaughan Road that we went to. 'Oh yes, you were with the one who fell through our record player,' she said. He fell through my bloody heart as well and made a right mess of it I can tell you because he resumed his ignoring of me after that. So back out in the cold world of Dennis not giving a shit about me, I had to get over it all once more.

Leda and I decided to move out of Grandma's (or Sainsbury's as we called it, so fond was she of that store) and back into Mum's again, now that we were on better terms with her. At this time a young guy called Paul, who just happened to be the son of Lemmy from 'Motörhead', was also lodging there in my old room. Paul was a tall willowy blonde and we actually called him 'Lincoln Continental', because although he had no driving license, he did have a large blue Lincoln Continental 'automobile'. He was very fond of it, though it broke down continually and consequently spent most of its life parked forlornly on the icy street. As Paul was in my spooky old room (where one night he thought he heard a ghost), I went into one of the new bedrooms in the never to be completed (by us) extension. This was a cheery space, painted yellow and it looked out onto the sad and wintry garden. There the trees that I used to climb up as a youngster, stood about like sentinels awaiting the next phase in their lives (which I have strong reason to believe, involved an encounter with a large chainsaw). I had used their fallen leaves so many Novembers to make the guys for Bonfire Night that had sat upon the fire resplendent in Dad's old stage clothes (after later selling the few we had left at Bonhams, the bonfire bit is an undertaking I now look back on with some regret).

Noisy firework parties had been a speciality carried over from the Neasden days when we'd had our bonfire in the back alley at Braemar Avenue and had roasted potatoes in the fire (not hedgehogs though, which was a suggestion made to us by the Nigerian trumpet player Mike Falana). In those far off 1960s days, the Beautiful People had floated about in voluminous swathes of fabric and long scarves, narrowly avoiding death by ignoring their *'Please keep this garment away from fire'* labels. Eric (Clapton) once brought the entire cast of The Royal Court Theatre with him, who then proceeded to traipse mud through the tiny kitchen until the white lino floor was black with it. Several thespians then began opening the kitchen cupboards saying to mum 'We are told this is where Liz keeps 'such & such" 'I am Liz' she replied!

Once in Harrow though, we went up market and purchased boxes of expensive fireworks from Brocks. Dad liked to spend the day digging deep holes in the lawn for the enormous mortar shells. At firework time, no one could see him at all for the smoke as old Gandalf did his bit and concerned females called out, 'Ginger are you okay?' through the murk.

Guests such as June Bolan and Madeleine Bell would gasp with delight at the grand finale of 'The Whistling Waterfall' that was strung across the children's climbing frame. This wonder of pyrotechnics shrieked loudly and lit the garden up as bright as day. Dad would then begin the clear up by throwing the dead fireworks into the flames and once an unexploded jumping cracker flew back out of the fire and landed down the front of his shirt. He ran around the garden swearing and a neighbour (which may even have been old 'Slipper of the yard', because he lived over the back there), leaned out of an upstairs window, dressed in a striped nightshirt and barked, 'Do you mind, I'm trying to sleep here!'

'And I'm fucking burning to death!' came the reply.

Then Denny Laine and Jack Bruce set off for a race round Harlesden in their Ferraris, during which I believe they got stopped by the police.

By 1985, the garden was forgetful of it's glorious past, as was the loft, which could be reached from a pull out ladder in a cupboard on the landing. It had once been Dad's workshop and he would stay up all night carving a wondrous totem pole thingy, until he put the chisel through his finger and woke the whole house up by shouting, 'get a tourniquet, get a tourniquet!' at three o'clock in the morning.

He also made a beautiful model Trimaran boat from plywood, complete with little cabins that had diddy Perspex windows (but unfortunately in a fit of pique my mother smashed it to smithereens with an axe). A drug addled artist mate of his had painted a rude mural of a naked woman on the white chipboard down one wall and for sinister reasons I failed to grasp, this caused many harrowing arguments to take place. But now the space lay quiet, with the old bench and vice still in situ and curls of wood shavings and empty Rothman's packets littering the floor. The wind moaned sadly and the high cobweb strewn window looked out over the wet rooftops of Sudbury Court Drive that angled steeply down towards the roundabout.

So Leda and I settled in for a brief spell and then someone decided to host a twenty-four hour music marathon at The Pumphouse in Watford, in aid of The Miners I believe. I turned up early, then went home and got changed in order to go to the good old 'Middlesex and Herts' (or 'Sex and Tarts') Country Club, up at Old Redding for Sandra's birthday. We met up at The Case is Altered pub and I immediately attracted a lot of hostility from the 'straights.' But in the club I had fun and even got accosted by someone half decent until Alison dragged me away.

It was a frosty night and I got dropped off back at The Pumphouse at 2.30 a.m feeling lively and looking like a Christmas tree. I met a mate in his camper van outside; I asked him who was in there and when he uttered the word 'Dennis,' I was gone like a flash of lightning, completely forgetting that I wasn't supposed to be talking to him. He wasn't too unfriendly, in fact he even invited me to sit with him and I was as ever cringingly grateful for those crumbs of attention from the rich man's table.

Leda was already there and she and Dennis got up on stage with their guitars and jammed. His bass had a large black number 'Five' stuck on it and he gave me a long look before he launched into a loud rendition of 'This Ain't No Party'. You're bloody right there mate. Nevertheless, I swooned away. Later on still, some heavy looking Hells Angels turned up and one of them came over and chatted me up beautifully. I mean just sitting there whilst somebody tells you are wonderful is certainly my idea of a good time. I had hoped Dennis might be jealous but to tell you the truth I don't think he even noticed.

# CHAPTER TWO
# Eviction

*'The only way is up'*
(Yazz)

On 29th January 1985 Mum came home in a dark mood because Basualdo was trying to evict us again on 7th February. Yet strangely even with that dire warning we all carried on as though nothing untoward was going to happen. On Saturday 2nd February we had another party. The neighbours reeled in disbelief as busloads of hippies and a sprinkling of punks rolled up and proceeded to make a lot of noise until the early hours. So the old place was packed and The Queen of the Punk Scene perched delicately on the large black leather swivel chair by the living room window.

In 1970 not long before he died, Jimi Hendrix had sat in that very same seat. I had been aware that we had a 'guest' that night and came downstairs for a good look at him. I peered in and asked for 'a glass of water' as you do. He quickly clocked me spying through the crack in the door and said, 'Hello', then beckoned me to go over and sit on his lap, which I did for about half an hour (yes, I've had many a drink bought for me on the strength of that one anecdote). Jimi struck me as a quiet, softly spoken guy.

By the time of this very last party, the famed eight foot long tropical fish tank in the lounge was half empty and devoid of life. The plastic miniature wreck and Perspex sculptures made by Dad protruded sadly from the dark scummy water. The riotous gathering surged on around it like a loud and jumbled epitaph to our lost years of glory.

The next day, I went over to see Robert's mother (my young lover from book one, now working as a polo groom in the USA). I often went to visit her whilst he was away. She didn't know what had been going on with us and assumed that we were 'just good friends' apparently. Though why she would think I'd bother with him if I wasn't after his body I have no idea. So I got the bus over to Ruislip and had tea with her; then I took our respective dogs out for a run over the common. As I walked, the sun sank down the pale clear winter sky and was replaced by a full moon that rose early and sailed brightly and hopefully along above the tops of the bare trees.

On the 6th February we were told that the bailiffs would be arriving to throw us out the next day. Yet still we carried on heedless of our fate and that night I went over to Alison's to celebrate her birthday. Sandra gave me a lift back for the last time ever to 49 Littleton Road, the house that had been our home for seventeen eventful years, but was about to be no longer.

Early on that February morning the bailiffs knocked upon the door. A dim-witted, surly and sombrely dressed 'Vogon' (see Douglas Adam's *Hitch Hikers Guide to the Galaxy*) barged his way into my lovely bedroom and said, 'Pack your stuff; you've got five minutes to get out.' This experience immediately made me think about more harrowing historical situations, where the innocent had been forcibly removed from their abodes. Those Repo-men, who followed orders under the guise of 'at least we've got a job' (because most of us didn't), were similarly affected by a total lack of empathy for their victims. We were scum to them and it was a cold morning devoid of humanity as Lincoln Continental and I stood out on the street with our belongings in black bin bags whilst a steady drizzle fell around us. Leda had been staying at her boyfriend 'Pike's' house in Hindes Road, but we had managed to get word to her. They got on a 182 bus, but poor Pikes, although he had the appearance of a person to whom chaos is commonplace, was clearly not as seasoned as us, because he repeatedly said, 'Oh my God I can't cope with your mad family', for the whole of their journey along the wet and windswept Watford Road.

At the house, Mum had by now been picked up bodily and thrown into the street. Then under no circumstances was she to be allowed back in to retrieve anything she might have forgotten and this may have been due to the way in which she was threatening to disembowel the very self-important looking individual standing guard at our front door. I however, managed to talk my way round him and locate some of the jewellery and trinkets that she had accrued in wealthier times. Soon the rain began to fall in earnest, so Leda and I took shelter in the garage amongst the various flotsam and jetsam of our past. Spare parts for Jensen FFs and Range Rovers reclined against the dusty walls along with old skateboards, hamster cages, orange pond lights, velvet curtains, balding pampas grasses and old quadraphonic speakers. Mr Estate Agent had followed us and he kindly and sympathetically imparted this information, 'You can't stand here, because this is no longer your property.' Leda picked up an old curtain rod and began feinting around him in the manner of someone fencing. 'Come on and fight for it!' She said.

We dearly wished that we had been living in medieval times and could rightfully defend our home by letting loose flights of arrows supplemented by cauldrons of boiling pitch expertly aimed from the upstairs battlements (shades of Python's *'fetchez la vache'*). The removal men arrived to empty the large house and so too did the local press to gleefully document our spectacular decline. The snooty neighbours that Janet and I had once waved at condescendingly from the window of our limousine had their long awaited revenge. As the beautiful antique furniture went out in winter's disgrace, I began musing on the glorious summer days when it had gone in. Out came the nineteenth-century dining table and chairs that Dad and I had gone down to Somerset on a hot day to collect. We had travelled in a lorry with Cream roadie Mick Turner at the wheel. Out came everything that our newfound riches had bought us.

By comparison to our Neasden maisonette, our new house situated at the bottom of Harrow Hill was enormous. It had four bedrooms and by the time of our ignominious departure that had risen to six. In 1968, it had been standing empty for quite a while and gave off a sinister air, surrounded as it was by an unkempt garden of man-height nettles. The local children had crossed the road to avoid the place because they said that it was haunted. But then a flurry of activity had ensued and the neighbourhood gossips announced that a pop star was moving in and all the walls were being painted different colours! It was true, all the colours of the rainbow, all over the place. Deep reds, pinks, purples, blues and greens adorned them in indiscriminate fashion. My bedroom was orange and yellow with sun coloured curtains covered with marigolds and I had a washbasin and a four-poster bed from Heals that cost £127. Dad stood on the newly acquired dining room table and painted the ceiling rose with a swirling rainbow that incorporated all the colours used in the house. Then he said he had a stiff neck.

But in 1985, the removal men disdainfully discovered a long unused kitchen drawer that was filled with syringes of various sizes. (I smiled in remembrance of the time at Heathfield's school when we'd had a craze for squirting water at each other through various implements and I had been by far the most popular with my comprehensive syringe collection from home!) Then Roy 'the get away driver' suddenly pitched up and managed to load most of our personal possessions into his van. He took us back to Grandma's. Mum had to wait for the police to come and they were quite decent and gave her a lift over to her uncle's place, as she sat innocently in their vehicle with a large lump of hash in her pocket. The incredible furniture that the burly men were heaving out so unceremoniously, would also have been lost to us forever had it not been for the great good fortune of Mum's secretarial job with the double glazing company. They allowed her to store it all in their warehouse at Havelock Place in Harrow. We went back to the house the next day in order to find our cat and we discovered her mewing piteously in the back garden, because of course the nice men had nailed up the cat door.

The truth is, that we were one amongst many families who were suffering the same fate at this time. It is well documented that the economic see-saw had created problems of negative equity and/or sudden redundancies that in turn had forced bewildered families into the bleak land of dole queues and bed and breakfast accommodation.

But the human cost of these statistics translates into the painful reality that everything you have known as personal to you and whatever you or your family have striven for is taken from you. Good old Locke's ideology of what constitutes as property is turned firmly upon its head. Leda went back that autumn and scrumped *our own* apples from the garden tree. When it went back on the market, it was our concrete pond with the bridge over it that Dad had built (complete with weird Perspex under water sculptures, coloured lights and the pump house decorated with an old camel's skull from the Sahara), that prospective buyers came to look at.

A strange white statue sat for many years in the front garden that was made by *my* Dad in 1965, as I sat and watched him in our sunny back garden in Neasden. (This consisted of a wire frame, which he overlaid with many layers of fibreglass and resin. Then he put a vacuum cleaner motor in the middle of it, which once upon a time revolved emitting showers of blue sparks as it did so.) Out the back, next to a flight of ornamental steps, stood 'Oscar;' yet another tall sculpture he had fashioned, resplendent in metal feathers, with eyes made out of binoculars and a great shining halo above his head. Oh yes, others happily reaped the rewards of our endeavour, but that is the way of the world, especially if you forget to play it the way the world says that you must.

Shaken but not stirred, we went back to Grandma's and continued to live life to the full even though we had nothing. Mum stayed with her Uncle in Kingsbury; then she rented various rooms here and there until she found one with a hippy mate of ours just up the road from us. We quickly settled into our new incarnation amongst the ranks of the outlawed and the dispossessed (or repossessed). Not one rich or famous person cared, noticed or even enquired about our fate (except for Screaming Lord Sutch, who lived nearby). Yet the poor and the mad, both young and old, offered us support and friendship.

There was some good news though and this was that pub opening times had been extended by half an hour, so that on weekdays we could now drink 'til eleven pm. That very night, I got the bus up to The Plough, where recent events had travelled fast upon the grapevine and our friends were quick to offer their sympathy. The next day, I met Mum down at the warehouse in Havelock Place to check on the state that our belongings had arrived in. It appears that some items had never arrived at all, such as a silver cut glass decanter given to us by Robert Stigwood and Mum's antique garnet necklace. Perhaps the nice removal chaps thought they deserved a bit of extra dosh? The rest of the furniture stood about looking very mournful in this vast, cold, dark and silent place and outside large flakes of snow began to fall. Snow, snow and yet more snow continued to blanket the land, whilst the wind howled through the long nights. Huge drifts were banked up against the trees in the park, sparkling in the moonlight as we trekked home from various social sessions, making Harrow look like 'The North Pole' to our stoned eyes.

One night as we were walking back with Hippy Phil, we came through the town centre where the empty shops were now being squatted by some Punks. On one building they had blanked out the name of the trader who had served us in happier days and daubed 'Afterbirths Unlimited' across it in blood red paint, which dripped ghoulishly down towards the vacant window. The old Somerton's department store had a first floor balcony along the length of its frontage and we spotted various mohicaned types running along it and ducking in out of the windows making monkey noises. Phil immediately responded in kind and they carried on a jungle-like dialogue that echoed round the deserted streets. Two tribes making contact in the wasteland.

Sadly The Bozo's split up, which I thought was most

inconsiderate of them, so there were to be no more nights dancing to them at The Plough. Then the warehouse got broken into and one of our television sets was stolen. Life was tough for us weirdos living in the organised straightness of our Grandparent's house. My brother Kofi was constantly falling out with them about the cat (?), so he went off and lived for a while on his drum riser at Acorn Studios. I had no cash and started taking my gold jewellery down to the pawnshop to get beer money. However, the sun finally came out and the spring arrived. Mum got some family allowance through and bought me a pair of shoes. We went to see Terry Gilliam's film 'Brazil' and were blown away by it. We also loved 'Bladerunner' of course.

On TV I never missed 'Top of The Pops' (in case Marc Almond was on!), 'The Tube' (what would Paula be wearing?), 'Only Fools And Horses', 'Minder', 'Max Headroom' and old Praed as 'Robin Hood'. There were also dramas such as, 'By the Sword Divided', 'Widows' and 'Inside Out' and as the year progressed I got hooked on the new soap 'Eastenders', as well as professing my amazement at the rise of Billy Bragg (see book one!). Leda and I began to get friendly with two girls who worked in the groovy hairdresser's and who did our hair for us on the cheap. This shop was called 'Memory Lane' and was very near to QOS (The Queen of the Scene)'s place in a little street in central Harrow that no longer exists. These girls said that they kept seeing the tall bleached blonde Marilyn (80's pop icon) look alike boy going in and out of QOS's all the time. We were all desperate to know more about him and we found out that his name was Marc so we spent ages gossiping about him. One of these two hairdressers was called Bee and she was an attractive, friendly girl with a sunny disposition, a black mohican and great sense of humour. The other girl was a right bitch. Nevertheless, she is still the best hairdresser I have ever had and Mum and I hadn't had one decent haircut between us since we last saw her in 1991 (so please come back all is forgiven). In addition to this, she looked fabulous with her long white hair extensions, but she had shaved her eyebrows off and drawn them in again high up and very black, so in private we usually referred to her as, 'The Flying Eyebrows.'

Flying Eyebrows had a very Gothic, girly, skinny boyfriend, who was always plastered in make-up. He had very long, black, backcombed hair and wore diaphanous black clothes. His name was Brian. I knew that if I were ever to meet him without his make-up on that I wouldn't recognise him at all. Flying Eyebrows and Brian used to go up to Camden a lot and there were postcards for sale everywhere depicting the two of them looking moody on a bench. Hairdresser Bee lived just around the corner from us in Blenheim Road, in a shared house with this guy Bondy and his girlfriend, another Jo. Bondy was being naughty quite a lot and seeing QOS. This caused Bee and Flying Eyebrows to hate QOS because they were jealous and not for any moral reasons, because everyone nobbed everybody else as much as possible in those days. Bondy like Pikes was my age, but the rest as I've already mentioned (in book one!), were five years younger. Leda and I began to go to Bee's to have our hair done and afterwards we'd go to the park and sit on the swings gossiping. These were my sort of people at last and they let us tag along. QOS had a sixties fancy dress party that we got invited to. She lived in the upstairs of a charming Victorian villa that the council were letting go to rack and ruin before they knocked it down. All the houses in her street had beautiful gardens and front doors that were inlaid with stained glass panels. QOS's flat was really her Mum's, but as she now lived elsewhere, the place was filled with Punks.

Wearing an original hand-made sixties pink wool mini skirt and matching jacket, (given to me back in Buckinghamshire by Jayne's lovely mum Mavis) I walked up a flight of stairs that were clad in moth eaten green carpet. They led up to a long dark landing where a large poster of the cast of The Rocky Horror Picture Show looked down from the wall and against this a very mean looking Goth with a phenomenal black mohican was leaning moodily. In the other rooms random Punks sported Afghan coats, headbands and beads in their interpretation of the swinging decade that they'd totally missed by being born right in the middle of it. Petula Clark's 'Downtown' was playing loudly and I was feeling quite happy in the kitchen and trying not to fall down the hole in the floor, when Dennis walked in, so I went home. I still wasn't as in with the Punk crowd as I desired to be, but all that changed on April 6th when Bee had a party.

# CHAPTER THREE
## Barbara's Fetish Party

*'Don't dream it, be it'*
(The Rocky Horror Show)

I knew that this was one that I had to mega dress up for so I really went for it. I wore the black jersey off the shoulder dress again and I put on more black make-up than ever, more studs, more chains and more hairspray. I was clanking about like Frankenstein's bloody monster and I snarled at myself in the hall mirror. Honestly, I feel that I've hardly looked better; artificial, aggressive, painted and predatory. Grandma had to go for a lie down. Pikes knocked on the door accompanied by the hippy girl whom Mum lived with and we walked just a few steps around the corner to Bee's at 106, Blenheim Road. Bee opened the front door and she was dressed in a black Basque, fishnet stockings and stilettos. This was more like it. Although it had been billed as a 'Fetish Party', it certainly did *not* mean bank managers in S&M gear! I was both amazed and delighted; a kid in sweet shop no less. Just walking into the front room was an experience. The young, the beautiful and the innocent were dressed up in the uniforms of sexual titillation and had come together (okay, no jokes) in their own spirit of camaraderie. Rows and rows of outlandish spiked-up hairdos meshed together, casting shadows like exotic flowers upon the opposite wall. Several very beautifully proportioned and heterosexual young men wore stockings and suspenders and they looked very good. Others ran the gamut of post apocalyptic style (not that it really would be without hairspray and electricity for hair-dryers). This ranged from a Phil Oakey look alike who lounged in one corner, his black-lined eyes gazing into those of his equally beautiful girlfriend, and what could have been most of the cast from the film, 'Mad Max 2'. It was a dressed up world of artifice and masks, concealing what? I had no idea. In another room, a six foot five giant dressed in leather, with green hair and needles through his earlobes offered me a light from a box of Swanvestas. The hippy girl who'd come in with us suddenly announced that the atmosphere was 'too aggressive' for her to handle and so she left. Bye.

The same Goth from QOS's sixties bash who had leaned so moodily against the wall, now sat silent upon a sofa and I took him again in from head to foot. He was very tall and his endlessly thin legs were wrapped in tight black jeans. His boots were pointed and adorned with silver spurs. His hands were strong and his nails were long. The fringe of his giant black mohican slightly obscured his dark brown kohl-rimmed eyes. He had a large hooked, hawk nose and a sensuous mouth. I made a few friendly approaches that weren't rebuffed. In the meantime, I also got talking with a girl that I'd often seen around the town, she had tall bleached blonde hair and her name was Linzi. This was the person who took the trouble to fully initiate me into the Punk circle. Linzi told me which pub it was that they all drank in and she said to come down anytime, as she would be there. After that, I went into the hall and noticed that some more hippy mates had turned up; they kept talking to me, but I wished that they would go away. I kept glancing upwards where two very cheeky young sods were sitting at the top of the stairs looking down at me. They were about eighteen; one was very broad, tall and clean looking, whilst his grubby, shaggy haired mate was short and slim. I knew they were taking the piss out of me because they'd never seen me before. In fact, they had decided with evil glee that with my goofy teeth I resembled Bugs Bunny and so they amused themselves by saying, 'Pesky wabbit,' every few minutes and laughing. But I didn't care about them. I just gave a bit of abuse in return and carried on with the job in hand. I went back to talk to the tall Goth. He was reticent, had a deep voice and he spoke very quietly. I enjoyed conversing with him about hairspray and the importance of umbrellas for keeping the mohican dry, so I guess it wasn't too intellectually demanding. Eventually, I took him back to Grandma's and we did it on the green rug next to the dining room fireplace. It was a small room and a bit of a squash with the heavy nineteen-twenties table legs and chairs getting in the way. He left at about five in the morning and he didn't ask for my phone number. I stood at the front door of 14 North Avenue and watched him limp away like a zombie illuminated in the street lamps glare as dawn came up above the suburban roof tops.

Walk, tall shadow into the memories of night
Melt the very darkness with your tall imposing height
Cross the ways that we once passed when lust fed passion's light
Walk on into the twilight world that reality can't blight.

Walk, tall shadow like a phantom on his way
Weave the story of that meeting like some fantasy astray
Follow the paths of some dimension other than today
To fading strains of lonely songs and music sad and strange to play.

Walk, tall shadow, like the miracle you are
Formed from fragmented shapes of dreams, so shaded
and bizarre
And brought to life upon my lips with tastes no alcohol
could mar
Stirred subtly in my questing soul, the musings of some
newborn star.

I had finally managed to live the dream and the fantasy
in my head had actually come to life. In the real world this
uber Goth's name was Greg, he was Greek (with a long
surname), and he lived in some flats called Drake Court
up in Rayners Lane.
The hippy girl who owned the house where Mum
stayed, was working in The Townhouse recording studios
at Shepherd's Bush and she invited us up there the next
night. Some ageing lothario that she knew waltzed in and
asked us if we fancied going with him to a nightclub called
'Gossips' in Dean Street. At first I wasn't very enthusiastic,
until I got in there and saw that it was packed full of
Punks. One seven foot corpse-like guy looked like a sort of
Keith Richards with lots of make-up on, whilst the music
was so loud that I was deaf by the time I got home and my
ear drums were still ringing the next day. Nevertheless I
was inspired and at last Pikes finally gave up the one
remaining style secret of the Punks, which was the mega
importance of Crimpers. With them you really could get
your hair very high indeed. It was Leda who first decided
to get the Bic razor out and go bald at the sides and I
quickly followed suit, with even my brother jumping on
the bandwagon for a spell. The baldness gave you more
space to take your make-up into and I drew on anarchy
signs or spider webs with black eye pencil.

Under the new regime, I would wash my hair and tease out all the old hairspray, which resulted in large congealed lumps appearing in the teeth of the comb. Then I would lather up some soap and put that on before drying my hair upside down and coating it with fresh hairspray. The next step was to crimp it all section by section, using more spray, which caused the irons to smoke as they became coated in burnt soap and hair lacquer. Then I'd backcomb it fiercely and shape it and keep spraying away using the hair-dryer to harden it to perfection. Most of us were easily getting through one giant can of Boots hairspray a week (no wonder there was a hole in the ozone layer). The mohican had to withstand the elements to a certain extent but in a high wind you could really feel it tugging at your roots and sometimes you would get a bit lop-sided. Having an umbrella with you at all times was of course essential. Dad had some sort of an attack about it and decided that I was a bad influence and he wrote, 'Get Leda out of Harrow' totally missing the point that it was all Leda's idea in the first bloody place! But being the oldest I suppose you always get the blame. He also said we were all 'mutants' with our outlandish style, so we laughed and went down to look at some photos of him in a Rock music book in W H Smith's. In this we saw him dressed in a Victorian jacket, with his hair in a high ponytail and his white flares looked as if they'd had a fight with his snakeskin patchwork boots. We thought about pots calling kettles black. With the moke in place, the next thing to do was take Linzi up on her offer and get myself tarted up and ready for a visit to Punk Mecca, 'The Royal Oak' in Harrow.

# CHAPTER FOUR
# Life at The Royal Beard

*'Big A little a, bouncing b.*
*The system might've got you but it won't get me'*
(Crass)

The Royal Oak on St Ann's Road in Harrow's town centre had once been known as The Gateway. Under that name it had been the biker's pub with the pennies in Perspex at the bar that I'd visited back in 1978/9. Now it was a Punk pub and the cool dudes still referred to it by its former name. Not much had changed inside, only the pennies had gone. It was a homely and cosy place, with two carpeted sections connected by a low step and it got very narrow at one end. The woodwork was dark and a fire burned in the grate in wintertime. There were train signs dotted about the walls and a set of red and green signals, hung drunkenly over the toilet door. I felt confident enough under ten tons of war paint and I saw Bee straight away. Then I met up with another girl I knew who, because of her later tendency to run off into the night crying, became known as Zola. Zola and I soon got very friendly and it was our habit of saying 'Jimmy Hill's Beard' about everything that we thought was a lie; that led to this place where most of our romantic successes (hardly any) and disappointments (loads) were played out; into becoming known by us as, 'The Royal Beard.'

Linzi from the party welcomed me warmly and Leda decided to reinvent *her* as a Jeeves and Wooster type character from the nineteen-twenties, called Pinz, who wore a monocle and flew about in a bi-plane with crates of Special Brew strapped to the wings. Pinz drank Special Brew by the bucketful and at Christmas for some years afterwards, she would come over and have her traditional green pint, which consisted of Special Brew with a liberal dousing of Crème De Menthe.  She had a brother Tim (known sometimes as 'Onion head' after his hair style) and a younger brother Matt who joined us as he got older. I then met Stripey Jayne, which is self-explanatory; she was a clever middle-class girl doing fashion and God knows what at college. Then there was Gary who was perhaps gay and did photography, art and picture framing and there was Duncan. Duncan got attached to my siblings, he played bass guitar and often jammed with them at Acorn Studios. He is one of the funniest people I have ever met, along with Pikes, Pinz and Big Lisa.

On this first night I also met up again with Adam (he of the green hair and the Swan Vestas at Bee's party), with QOS, Seamus, Slimy, and some old mates of David's. So this is where they all hung out. Suddenly, the door swung open and in limped 'Umbrella Man' the Goth himself. He entered cautiously out of the wet and windy April night and shook the rain from his brolly. Then he stopped to blow his nose on an enormous white handkerchief. (Very soon his limping gait led to him becoming known as Peg Leg).  He looked rather embarrassed when he saw me and ran away when I tried to speak to him.

After this, we started to mix the crowds up even more. Goths and Punks ended up in the Tandoor and hippies infiltrated The Royal Oak. That definitely increased everyone's chances of getting to and hearing about whatever parties were on and there were at least two every weekend and sometimes even three on one night. Life got busier by the moment, I acquired more friends and became Queen if not of the coolest inner circle then at least of my own scene. Being a big fish in a little pond suited me perfectly and being older led to me having to discharge agony aunt duties to the young and confused, God help them. Once I got well established, I would only have to put a cigarette to my lips and at least ten male hands would appear with matches and lighters at the ready. This is the life. Many of us were signing on and those of us with surnames in the A's and B's would meet up on a Monday morning in the queue outside the dole office. We would ring round whenever there were postal strikes and let each other know when there would be trouble or delays in getting our very important Giros. Other people were at college and some of them even had jobs, shock horror! For a vast majority though 'Work' was the four-letter word. Duncan did get a job after college and on receipt of his first pay packet he spent a jubilant evening at the 'Beard' and ended up lying unconscious under a picnic table. Later when he got the sack, he said, 'Oh, I didn't realise that you had to go in *everyday*'!

Other bods quietly did very well indeed out of life (including Duncan); some were essentially normal but with Punk style and some were fuck ups plain and simple, ending up as junkies, or in mental institutions or in the grave, and quite often a combination of all three. Therefore, this new scene represented a microcosm of the real world with all its hierarchies, petty squabbles and disappointments, yet at the same time, occasional enemies aside, it offered us all a unique and cohesive, extended familial structure, one in which we knew and understood something that no outsiders did. What that is exactly, I can't explain, but if you were there or have experienced similar then you know where I'm coming from. For the Bakers, it was life without Father, and as we'd always been completely dominated by his fame and his desires and dramas, we had no idea what our own wants might be. Chaos was all that we had ever known; therefore any attempts to restore us to order were inevitably viewed with suspicion.

On a typical summer's evening in '85, I'd come out of the front door in West Harrow and breathe in the familiar fragrances of roses and exhaust fumes as I walked along. At the end of Vaughan Road stood a high wall of yellow brick and I stopped there to wait for Pinz and Tim. My mohican was lacquered up to its artistic apex, my face was carefully painted and my hands were heavy with the weight of the many rings upon them. Very soon, around the corner of the little road that joins Vaughan to Butler; two yellow mohicans came bobbing. They were sharing a can of Special Brew, and as they approached I could hear the familiar jangling of Pinz's armful of silver bangles. We walked over Roxborough Bridge, pausing to lean upon the black brick of the parapet and admire the sprawling arms of an orange sunset as it reached out over the ruddy rooftops and reflected on the rails that snaked off towards North Harrow. Then we crossed the road at a little island, marched down the steep Roxborough steps and through a scrubby flowerbed, whilst the leaves of a great copper beech tree whispered above our heads. On we went, around the corner of our changing townscape, through the brick dust of the latest demolitions, over the builder's planks and under the scaffolding of the new town going up. Suddenly The Oak hove into view, all white walls, painted signs and hanging baskets. The windows were set with bottle glass and bulged as if they graced a seventeenth-century galleon. In front of the pub our crowd sat out on the picnic tables and dozens of different brightly coloured hairstyles nodded over their pints like the plumes of some fantastic birds.

*'Do you remember the good old days*
*before the ghost town?'*
('Ghost Town', The Specials)

As time went on, I would often meet up with Zola along the route. I would call for her at her house, next to West Harrow station with its (now long gone) crab apple tree in the front garden (nice jam). As we walked Harrow-wards along Vaughan Road we passed a terraced house that had a large oil painting displayed in the front room. As there were no net curtains, we could see in clearly and the picture had a light above it. We invented a superstition that if the picture wasn't lit up then we were in for a successful evening and vice versa. Therefore, if things went disastrously wrong, we'd say, 'Oh well, it's because the picture was lit up!'

Leda and I settled into the little back bedroom at Grandma's once again and I had posters of Jim Morrison and John Taylor (in full make-up) upon the wall. We weren't great at being tidy then, belonging to the Quentin Crisp school of housework, which is something like, *'After the first four years the dust doesn't get any worse'.*

Great balls of fluff appeared on the glass top of the 'thirties, kidney-shaped dressing table and curls of eye pencil shavings rolled about between the pots of eye shadow and cold cream. We did have the occasional cleaning fit, or should I say Leda did?

Despite our personal mess, we adopted a fairly green ideology concerning the planet, which resulted in many of us Punks trying to find aerosols with no CFC's in and we bought planet friendly washing up liquid and stuff; how holy! The whole Robin Hood thing had also inspired Leda to try and make an enormous bow, so that she could lurk about on Harrow Hill shooting arrows at the baddies. She found a large piece of Yew wood up in the graveyard and proceeded to spend hours sanding it down and seasoning it with linseed oil, which she also managed to spill over most of my clothes. When it was finished, she attached some green garden string to either end and drew it back to test its strength, whereupon it immediately snapped in half. We spent a lot of time up in that graveyard and I wrote loads of poetry up there, aware of course that Lord Byron had done so before me, though it goes without saying that his efforts were somewhat superior. We would look down and try imagine the views that he had had long before the countless redbrick terraces had come to march in serried ranks across the old hayfields of Middlesex. Leda got her guitar out and we resurrected an old poem that I'd written back in '83 and we made a song to it. It is a sort of Betjeman-esque lament for the past (wholly inspired by his brilliant 1973 TV programme, 'Metroland') and just gives you an idea of where our heads were at:

Mystic dreams of long dead places,
Sun on hair and smiles on faces,
Meadows wide and green across the land.
Where once were fields of meadowsweet,
Now stands an ugly, busy street
And houses in profusion hand in hand.
Broken bottles old and new,
Paved gardens where the cowslip grew,
A new tomorrow dwindling into smoke.
Oh, you meads that once were here

Your beauty's gone for good I fear,
As under heavy concrete now you choke.
Where have the drowsy summers run?
The river glinting in the sun,
The laughing children running through the grass.
The horses fording through the stream,
Their rider's buttons all agleam,
Who thought that such as this would come to pass?
Metal monsters belch their fumes
Past bored teenager's gaudy plumes,
Destroying every season that may come.
'Til we are left with yesterday,
A little lane on winding way
And rosy Hawthorns in the setting sun.

It was a hippy moment man! But the hippies were getting old now and the angry youth were all set to do some shouting. Down in the town new graffiti began to appear on walls, street signs and pillar-boxes. It said, 'Bean', 'Nig', 'Hig' and 'Tufty' all over the place; early instances of tagging I guess. Other interesting daubs proclaimed, 'Curl up and Die', 'Smile and be Damned' and later in the year my own particular favourite, 'Fuck Christmas, God is Dead'! I was soon to meet these 'taggers' in person. One of them (the fabulous Tufty) got cross with me in the 'nineties for identifying him in an article that I wrote about graffiti for a local newspaper. He thought it would upset his mother or something which was a bit concerning coming from such a paragon of naughtiness. In fact, the editors completely ruined what I was attempting to turn into a bit of a subversive story stating that there were social reasons for graffiti and that it could have significance. They were targeting a holy audience of disapproving old middle-class grannies so I couldn't even hint that I thought it was quite cool. (Anyway, sorry Tufty for trying to make a living out of your youthful indiscretions, I still think you're the bee's knees.) I continued to meet so many people when out and about that just popping into Harrow felt like going to a party.

Camden Lock market was another important place to visit and it was there that I had three more holes pierced in my right ear, bought anarchy badges, a studded dog collar and had my photo taken by Japanese tourists. Yet it was 'The Royal Beard' that became the centre of our soap opera of a life, in much the same way as the fictional Queen Vic or The Rover's Return. Although we did occasionally venture further afield to places like the real Queen Vic at Ealing Common or The Moscow Arms in the Bayswater Road. We travelled about a bit for gigs as well.

Then I met a girl called Sharon and she got me into more hardcore music like 'Crass', 'Conflict', 'Generation X' and the early Adam Ant stuff and she raved over a band called Flowers in the Dustbin. Cooler factions went off to see bands like 'The Ramones', 'UK Subs', 'Dead Kennedys' and 'Nick Cave and The Bad Seeds' etc, whilst others followed 'The Damned' and later on, 'The Cure'. Sham 69 sang, *'Questions and answers, honesty, lies / yes, no you can't, but you can and you know why'* and we sang along with them. Basically, we didn't want anyone anywhere telling us what to do. Tufty later said that,'We had no role models.' And Nig said that he just wanted, 'To piss people off'.

I suppose that in some ways we resembled the well-known and much earlier 'Bromley Contingent' that had included the likes of Boy George, Siouxie Sioux, Billy Idol and the 'face' 'Catwoman' amongst others. Like them, we spawned our own (quite) well-known faces. That Kirk geezer from 'Spear of Destiny'/'Theatre of Hate' used to drink in The Beard and Leda was friendly with Jamie, the bass guitarist in 'The Cult' ('She Sells Sanctuary') and his girlfriend Dot. But at Zola's house we listened to tamer stuff like 'Echo and The Bunnymen' and 'The Waterboys' and she even got me into a most non Punk Simon & Garfunkel track from aeons past called 'American Tune.'

*'I don't know a soul that's not been battered,*
*don't have a friend who feels at ease*
*I don't know a dream that's not been shattered*
*or driven to its knees'*

However, we danced about at parties to The Clash and The Pistols and we shouted to such great songs as 'White Riot' and 'Babylon's Burning.' So my taste was eclectic to say the least and not quite as in tune with the idea of absolute chaos as you may imagine. The dictionary explains the word 'Anarchy' as one meaning *'absence of government'* followed by *'disorder and confusion'*, when in fact the last two words are not what it meant to many of us. My badge said, *'No Gods, No Masters'* and I found a sound advocate of this kind of system in Ursula Le Guinn's novel 'The Dispossessed'. Of course it was all naïve and unworkable stuff, but young people were invented to try and explore different avenues and to think that they can change things. So we held on tight to these fragmented and half-baked theories, whilst at the same time continuing to pursue a hedonistic and frenetic lifestyle like those on the brink of war. Our war was probably the onset of adulthood (though I had already got there) and responsibility. Hardly anybody agreed with the 'get a good job, meet someone, get engaged, get a mortgage, get married, have children, have grand children and die' sort of thing. We actively fought against it for as long as we could, without of course having any clear alternative to it in mind apart from getting shit-faced every day!

One night, I dragged dear Pinz with me to a 'disco' that was being held at a place called 'Moritz'. This was actually at Wealdstone Football Club and now it is a Tesco store. Yes all types of entertainment have now (you may have noticed) been replaced by shopping (or eating). Anyway, when we got there we were at first horrified to find a disco full of Wedgies, but then we met up with the hippy lot and a band played which starred Dennis on bass and even at that late date, ten months or so after our first encounter, I thought secretly that he looked remarkably sexy for an old man. I then proceeded to chase him about all evening as he ran away. Eventually I gave up and Pinz and I walked home in various states of lunacy and disrepair. We had several mad routines that we'd follow on our walks home. If Pinz didn't have her brolly and it started raining she'd put a carrier bag over her head. Then we'd run along the top of the wall outside Bradstowe House saying we were the SAS, or Pinz would pretend to snort the white lines in the road.

Bradstowe House (now demolished) was at that time a DHSS office and naughty folks would post the gherkins from their MacDonald's through the letterbox. Meanwhile, Pikes and Leda broke up and The Bell came and took me out a couple of times. Once we went together to see some old married friends from Chalfont St Giles, but they as well as many others just couldn't handle me as a punk at all. There was a party up that way and even old hippy Alan told us off for enjoying ourselves (though Jimmy Carp joined in). Normal folks everywhere gave us a lot of abuse. Once I got stuck on a train full of straight commuters and they gave me funny looks all the way home. You could never walk past a school playground without getting some serious stick and one day, whilst innocently walking along, some bloke shouted, 'If you were my daughter I'd set fire to you.'

We never went down the pub when there were football or rugby matches on because you could guarantee that it would be full of 'Beer Boys' as we called them, hell bent on giving us grief. Some local hard nuts also drank down there, namely a bloke called Scots Eddie who was always beating his unfortunate victims over the head with bar stools. One of his cronies was giving poor Pinz a hard time one night, so she went into the loos, came out with a bar of soap, dropped it in his beer and said,

'My Mum says that if you use bad language you need to have your mouth washed out with soap.' Mr 'Very 'ard Indeed (not)' then retaliated by pouring the pint over her head. Ooops, he was a mate of the Governor, so we got chucked out!

Then Pinz got into a brief and tear-filled relationship with Adam and Peg Leg acquired a very beautiful girlfriend. She was a tall, sweet natured and graceful Goth named Alison. Even The Bell came down the pub and seriously lusted after her, which did wonders for my self-esteem I can tell you. A lot of activities found me echoing the trials of Arthur Dent in Douglas Adam's creation, 'Hitch Hiker's Guide to the Galaxy,' and by that I mean that I met lots of people who I *'tried and totally failed'* to get off with. I began writing to the Richard guy from the Edgware parties and he occasionally managed to reply. But most of the other eligible men had apparently been earmarked by QOS, which means that they were definitely off limits to the likes of me. It would have been like committing social suicide to tread on her toes. Tall Marc however, became a friend and one night he said he had wanted to speak to me the previous evening but had thought that The Bell was my boyfriend, to which I replied, 'Do me a favour, he's got a moustache'!

There was also a very pretty gay boy we knocked around with for a while. Some were and some weren't but pretended to be at that time. It was very cool to be unspecific about your gender preference in those days (way ahead of the game), which really is no bad thing and I heartily approved of very hetero guys trying hard to be camp. It definitely helped them to pull girls. Anyway, there I was just getting nicely settled in with my new crowd, when Robert came back.

# CHAPTER FIVE
# Men in Make-Up

*'I'm a hungry mohican, I've got a razor blade smile*
*so don't come near me, I've got a singular style'*
('Regrets', Eurythmics)

This can only have ended in disaster, but I felt I needed to give it a try. Robert's Mum had called me up and asked me to go and see her. So I got the bus over there and she gave me a glass of wine and left the room. The next moment there was Robert standing in front of me. The intervening six months had turned him into a bronzed and Americanised youth looking like something straight out of Miami Vice, whilst I in stark contrast had become a Gothic nightmare shaped in the harsh climes of an English winter. However, he was very attentive which was most welcome. I immediately took him down the pub where all the girls admired my latest pretty acquisition and even Peg Leg who hadn't yet got together properly with Gothic Alison, looked a bit surprised.

But Robert hated my black hair and make-up and begged me to change it back to something more girly. He called me 'The Bride of Dracula', whilst I found his sun kissed healthiness a bit of a let down compared to the silent, wintry watchfulness of Peg Leg. He repeatedly insisted that my look was just a façade that concealed the real me, whereas I was pretty insistent that it was in fact, the other way around. I don't think that Robert knew what to make of my mad crowd either.

Bee had got a new bloke. It was the tall one of the two cheeky buggers from the stairs at her party. His name was Tris and Robert and I met him on the bus the next day and chatted to him. He and Bee dressed alike and always had matching mohicans, sometimes orange, sometimes blue, etc, which was quite sweet really. I wondered if I could get Robert to change a bit. I was deeply in love for about three days. Oh yes, this was the one. April snow was blowing about in the freezing streets as Robert and I went off to the pub and then drifted along arm in arm to a party. Peg Leg stood like a sentinel sad and all alone and I felt a bit mean. On the short walk to the bus station, Seamus dropped an empty plastic cider bottle and immediately two officers of the law appeared and gave him a hard time, which prompted me to shout out, 'Haven't you got anything better to do in the evenings?' and Robert was desperately trying to shut me up. The poor police didn't know when they were well off then did they? Just a few middle-class wallys with silly hairdo's dropping some litter isn't much compared to what they have to deal with now is it? Serves them right.

Anyway, we got the bus down to Wealdstone for this party. Robert and I were all over each other and Peg Leg told his friend that he was depressed about it. I ended up sitting in a circle with Peg Leg and Robert on either side of me and I went on to conduct a 'Handsomest Man in the Room' competition that saw Robert coming first, gay and pretty Richard second, Peg third and Seamus fourth. Seamus took umbrage at this and said he thought he was better looking than Peg Leg but I had to disagree.

After the party, Adam, Pinz, Robert and I decided to walk up and get a cab. Peg Leg was also leaving so I cheered him up by asking him to come with us. There we were, a motley bunch, walking up the road past Wealdstone station, minding our own business, in the early hours of a cold morning. On the opposite side of the road we espied a group of drunken 'Casuals' coming along looking so smart in their Pringle jumpers and they soon spotted us lot. There were of course now no police to be seen anywhere and consequently we started to get a bit nervous. Peg Leg at once became the prime target of a pathetic wanker who ran across the road to us shouting, 'What do you fucking look like you freaks?' etc, over and over in a very menacing manner.

We said nothing and just kept on walking, but then this guy threw a punch at Peg Leg and I heard it connect to his jaw with a mighty 'thwack'. Nobody did anything, so I screamed, 'Don't you fucking touch him!' at the top of my voice and they did scarper.

For some reason that I will never know, we just kept on walking and nothing else happened. (Adam told me off because he thought I could've made things worse and I was upset by that; but about eleven years later Peg Leg himself actually thanked me for my outburst.) As a result of that punch, poor old Peg Leg soon had a huge mark appearing on his lovely face and when we parted at West Harrow I gave him a kiss and a few Marlboros to take home for the morning. He disappeared slowly and sadly off towards Rayners Lane holding a large umbrella at his side.

I was well in with The Flying Eyebrows as well at this time and the next day I went with her to a place in the Finchley Road where she got a tattoo done. In those days it was quite rare for girls to have these and therefore they were regarded as an outrageous statement, unlike nowadays when they are commonplace. I also had dinner one evening with her and Brian and we watched this disturbing TV docu-drama thing called 'Threads'. This was about what would happen in a normal suburban community if they dropped an atom bomb up the road. The whole cosy Thatcher and Reagan trip had worried liberals and lefties reaching for the smelling salts and believing that our unpleasant demise in the fall out of a nuclear winter was imminent. Life was highly coloured by this threat, much the same as it was in the sixties with the knock on effect of The Bay of Pigs malarkey. Seeing as I have survived so far, I now tend to (perhaps unwisely) dismiss all subsequent concerns in that area as being a load of media induced hysterical piffle. Anyway, back in '85, Flying Eyebrows dyed my hair again for me and shaved the sides and I knew Robert was going to hate it. As I'd predicted, Robert loathed my hair and I thought that at least Peg Leg liked the way I looked. However, one afternoon Robert did allow me to do his make-up for him so that cheered me up a bit.

My mate Alison, the teacher from 175, had bought a tiny upstairs flat in a terraced house in West Harrow. She was off on holiday and asked me to stay there for the duration to look after her cats and to give me the chance of a bit of freedom from 'The Dynamic Duo' (our Grandparents). Straight away, Robert said he didn't think he'd be able to stay there with me because now he'd passed his driving test his parents expected him home every night and this did not go down too well with me. The poor thing was only little and didn't know what he was getting into. Incurring my displeasure in this way was bound to have unfortunate repercussions. I went off and got drunk. I wanted to see Peg Leg but he wasn't there. Seamus was though and he was still unhappy about coming fourth in The Handsomest Man competition.

The next evening, I invited some folks back from The Royal Beard including Peg Leg. Robert was with us and

Adam was hassling me to hurry up, as there were a lot of Rugby fans in the pub. They had been insulting us for most of the night and there had already been a fight that resulted in someone getting glassed, so we needed to get away before they did. We all got back to Alison's safely and carried on drinking. It got late and more intimate and Robert fell asleep. Peg and I, who had been talking most of the time, then started kissing and I followed him into the kitchen.

'What about Robert?' he asked.

Oh sod Robert; it's you I'm after. Is what I really meant when I said that things, 'weren't going too well with us'. Men, honestly!

We stopped short of the deed because Robert was there and Peg shuffled off once more into the dawn after promising to come and see me on the following Monday. I sustained myself by catching glimpses of Marc Almond on 'Top of the Pops' (this has got to stop). Bee and Flying Eyebrows continued to slag off QOS for nicking all the best men. Scots Eddie had a fight one night and there was blood everywhere. Leda and I got a lift to one party in the back of a van, where we squashed in with Pikes and his new girlfriend. We found ourselves zooming along past Peg Leg who was walking along in the same direction and Pikes leaned out of the window and shouted, 'Look, there's Super Goth!' But he never bothered to visit me as promised.

Then QOS had a surprise party for Marc. I managed to conduct a brief flirtation with the Phil Oakey look alike guy from Bee's bash and he told me that he thought I was only nineteen, which pleased me mightily. As usual, this party soon degenerated into total chaos, helped in some measure by my own disparate (or desperate even) collection of followers who had got very drunk. Zola leaned on a mirror in QOS's bedroom, which fell on her head and broke and Pinz was once again crying over Adam. They were definitely looked down upon by QOS's inner circle of the ultra cool; who as far as I could gather appeared to consist of QOS, Marc, Bondy, Little Tris, Mitch, J.J, Adam, Beautiful Brigitte and Little Brigitte, Oakey look alike, Pikes, Big Lisa, a couple known as Janet 'Blue hair' and her boyfriend Pete and some others. In addition to this lot, there were also two 'cool' girls who I felt were very hostile to me, and Pinz already referred to one of them as Yawn. (The other one did eventually become a good friend but old Yawn really was a stupid cow who thought she was bloody marvellous and of course everyone fancied her, which might have had something to do with the fact that I couldn't stand her.) These two were in the kitchen, sitting round the hole in the floor and talking to an attractive, big-nosed, black-haired guy, later known to many of us as 'H please Bob' (in part reference to his drug of choice). Now 'H please' Bob's father happened to be a celebrity showbiz presenter. Seamus stepped in to the room just at the very moment that the girls began going on about this famous connection and so he pricked up his ears and let slip with, 'Nettie's got a famous Dad as well.' They turned to me disinterestedly and looked down their noses, 'Oh, who is that then?' they asked with disdain. I enjoyed the lull that ensued once Seamus had informed them. Well, if you must have a celebrity parent then at least chose a decent one.

I very quickly became aware of the existence of many other Punk-ish groups that lurked about in our shady suburbs. There was a 'hardcore' factor that inhabited/hung around various squats and some of them also dabbled in heavier drugs. This lot were Nig, Hig, Tufty, 'Bean', Gaz, Simon, Pinner, and Pongo, amongst others. A really entrenched and older junkie faction seemed to be in some way affiliated to the couple who ran the hairdressers. There were two junkie Dave's (one of whom was gay and had 'allegedly' been a victim of the serial killer Dennis Nielsen but had managed to escape) and two junkie Pete's, in addition to a tall 'Lurch' and a lanky 'Bones'.

Another couple of hopeless cases were Del and Mel. Del was stunning to look at and he strongly resembled the character 'Slaine' from the comic '2000AD.' Mel was a total disaster with the vestiges of what once had been a remarkable beauty clinging about her ravaged face and she had a whiny addict's voice. Her junkie father was found dead one day, rolled up in a carpet, in a derelict house at the back of Harrow Met Station. Apparently, the spaced-out brigade had been walking over him for weeks and were only alerted to his unfortunate state when a finger dropped off! Even worse, were some very dangerous and unsavoury characters indeed, who eventually got done for the murder and GBH of their own kind (one stabbed his mate to death and the other, a good-looking, yet evil boy, set about his stepfather with a hammer for allegedly turning him over in a drugs deal).

As always, these folks moved about between the various social groupings and if someone got messed up on smack they'd join the junkies, or if they wanted to squat they'd get in with the 'hardcores' (that's if they could win Nig over) etc, etc. Others like Tris, floated about at the more respectable end of things.

Tris had a close mate who was also named Tris and inevitably they became known as 'Big Tris' and 'Little Tris'. Little Tris was a drummer, just like his mate and for a long while he had a very attractive girlfriend called Mikki. But he also got mixed up with QOS, as did just about everyone. Of more interest to me, was the fact that

Big Tris had an older brother called Steve. He was intelligent (got a degree), was tall and skinny with a lovely freckled face and long ginger hair. He came across as a really animated, sexy and interesting bloke. Consequently, I had my eye on him quite early on I have to admit (not that he noticed me of course). Steve liked to tell the tale of how he once rounded the corner of a sunny and long ago demolished street in the town centre, only to find that Pete, Tufty and Nig in full punk attire were relaxing on a three-piece suite in the middle of the road and nonchalantly reading the Sunday papers.

The hippies had another party and Hippy Phil got spectacularly out of it after helping himself to most of Tim's bottle of Ouzo. He then tried and failed to chat everyone up and when he ran out of candidates he went and passed out face down in the garden. Pinz attempted to leave, but for some reason she ended up spending the next half an hour with her face pressed up against the outside of the front room window pulling ridiculous faces for the entertainment of all those who were still sober enough to notice. I began to liken the time it took me to get ready to go out as to that of getting a horse ready for a show and I wondered if I'd have got a prize for the best turned out (or not)? Meanwhile Pinz would be getting ready at her house, drinking special brew, spraying hairspray, smoking fags and then leaning out of the window to prevent an early death from asphyxiation. I'd often pop into see Bee en route and she'd do my hair and we'd go up the pub together. One night I accidentally met up with the old John Lyon gang and they laughed their heads off in disbelief at my transformation. I felt sorry for them actually.

Mum's landlady decided to liven Pinz and I up one evening by inviting two guys she knew to come and take us out and they were very plonkerish and old looking for twenty-six. One was a tall and ginger Kiwi called, strangely enough, 'Kiwi' and the other was a small and mouthy lad named 'Mad Eyes.' He was quite amusing I suppose when you're drunk on a Sunday afternoon with nothing better to do. He kicked off the proceedings by taking the piss out my hair for ages until he finally got used to it and calmed down a bit. But then he upset Mum (not that hard to do) so we went off to The Roxborough and then they took us to their local, which was the now (as usual) demolished 'Prince of Wales' in Kingsbury (its a supermarket now, wouldn't you know?). These odd lads paid for all the cabs and booze etc, so Pinz and I were more than happy to tag along. Eventually however, boredom compelled me to seriously flirt with and chat up the 'Kiwi' bloke for my own amusement and he predictably got really excited and thought that his luck was in. The only sounds that he seemed capable of uttering were the phrases, 'Goddammit!' and 'Fuck it!' repeatedly until I began to wonder if he were in actual fact a robot whose tape had got stuck. Nevertheless, if he'd looked really, really good, then he would've been in with a chance. But he didn't and so Pinz and I soon decided to get a cab back to the safety of The Beard, where I ran over to Stripey and Tim and implored them to save me from this maniac. Finally, thank the Lord, he got the hint and disappeared. I met up with Leda who had my brother Kofi's bike with her and on the way home we stopped to pick the dog up from Mum's. I pulled sibling rank on her and commandeered the cycle, then I set off riding unsteadily along the street, singing, 'Raindrops keep falling on my head' very loudly, *a la* Butch Cassidy. Then I narrowly missed crashing into parked cars and lamp posts, as the dog ran in front of me barking madly and Leda ran breathlessly behind shouting, 'Slow down!'

Don't say the four letter word, but sometimes you do

need money, so as well as doing a bit of leafleting for the double-glazing company boys, I was also doing some cleaning for Janet's Mum at her house in Sudbury Court Drive. There I would get a free lunch, a glass of sherry and £7.50, which I thought was a very good deal. Janet's family were/are Christians in the truest sense of the word and they always helped me and never once judged me or mentioned my strangeness. (Only old Nana would sometimes remark good-naturedly that she wondered what colour my hair would be on my next visit.) These jobs, coupled with the odd trips to the pawn shop helped me keep going until Giro day, but I would often get to the end of the week with about 2p in my purse. Nevertheless, Pinz and I could still manage a storming night out on just a couple of quid in those days as whoever was in funds would be more than happy to buy the other one a beer. Life isn't about money though chaps, it's about 'lurve' and I had to keep on searching for it, no matter what.

QOS's nineteenth birthday came along in June and this momentous date was always celebrated in an elaborate style. As you may have already gathered, just about every young buck in the vicinity was in love with her, or had been, or hoped to be and she somehow managed to carry on several illicit liaisons at once without even incurring that much flak about it. She gave off the air of being simultaneously worldly wise and girlishly silly, she snapped her fingers in the face of authority and convention. Her hairstyles varied with her Gemini moods and her clothes were fabulous creations of satin and velvet, thrown together anyhow from the dusty rails of thrift shops and the chaotically laden tables of local jumble sales. Her hems and seams more often than not were held together with safety pins or sewn up tight with frenzied stitches. She wore opulent strands of glistening pearls and rings of flashing onyx and marcasite and beautiful shoes that she had discovered in London's seedier second-hand markets. Consequently, she was often impeded in her forward motion as another heel came adrift or a stocking fell down and then her language became quite as colourful as her attire. In her ripped vintage garments she became a slide show of various quirky twentieth-century characters that had been culled from fact and fiction. Mia Farrow as 'Daisy' in 'The Great Gatsby', Liza Minelli as 'Sally Bowles', 'Factory Girl' Edie Sedgewick and Audrey Hepburn as her incarnation of 'Holly Golightly' in 'Breakfast at Tiffany's'. It was a strange coincidence that her father turned out to be the jazz drummer Johnny Armatage that my parents had known in the early sixties. He and her mother had moved into the same grotty flat in Bassett Road, Ladbroke Grove that our embryonic family had just vacated. Like me, she had eventually ended up in Harrow when her parents parted and then along with quite a few others, she had become the Punk scourge of Whitmore High School in South Harrow (whilst the Wealdstone contingent had caused mayhem within the portals of the notorious Hatch End High).

On QOS's birthday, the sunlit apartment fairly overflowed with gifts of every kind and her mother had furnished the front room with tall and tottering piles of presents. Once these had been torn into, a favoured few of us sat drinking and smoking amongst the gaudy discarded wrappings and were entertained by the wit and brio of our birthday girl. I felt incredibly honoured to have gained such an entry into the hallowed circle because it indicated that I had finally arrived.

*'I'm in with the In Crowd...'*
(Mamas and Papas)

The room fell silent momentarily and QOS who knew all about my horsey life, suddenly burst out with, 'Do you know that Nettie picks up pooh with her bare hands?' in her high little voice. The prettiest men in Harrow looked aghast. Well they do now. It was time for party games and QOS was keen for us to play her favourite one, 'Postman's Knock'. To be honest, I've never really been much of a fan of party games (except for 'Spin the Bottle' of course). Fortunately, Janet 'Blue Hair' wasn't in to it either, and our mutual eye rolling at the prospect of such impending silliness became a major factor in our burgeoning friendship. It is true to say (and many have said it), that this whole 'Punk' ideology was the first time that boys and girls had an equal scene together and Janet was the embodiment of all that I most respected in a girl of our time. Her deep blue hair was crimped and either swept up high or left long and her use of make-up was highly original, often incorporating a squared off, black, white and blue chequer-board effect. She definitely had a bit of a leaning towards a 1950s style of dress and was into Elvis and Doris Day. But although Janet drank and mucked about and partied with all the rest of us, she never lost her cool or got dramatic and she remained forever wise and calm in the face of all adversity. She may have been up all night and yet she quietly attended college, gained all her qualifications and went on to work for the NSPCC and then for Greenpeace; a job that much later took her to Sydney, Australia.

So there we all were on QOS's birthday and things started to get lively. The gifts from her Mum had included several boxes of Tampons, which were unfortunately soon plundered by silly people who soaked them in drink and threw them in the air where they remained stuck to the ceiling for ages afterwards. Seamus had gone out and bought risqué items from a sex shop, such as glow in the dark condoms and coconut flavoured 'nipple drops'. QOS came over with them and anointed me and I got into a game that resulted in me having a bit of fun with Tim, Pikes and another young boy. He had spiky bleached blond hair; great brown doe eyes, several tattoos and I'd been eyeing him up all day. This was Gaz, our very own blond bimbo. He later became a hopelessly addled addict who as a last resort was injecting smack into his knuckles, but in these early days he still retained his charming and tousled air of innocence. Flavoured naughty drops obviously have their uses because I was thrilled when Gaz and I started getting off with each other and he turned out to be a very good kisser indeed.

I am so tired and I long to sleep
Where dreamer's walk and in some shadow's breath
To find contentment in one kiss to keep
Pressed forever in the sweet embrace of death

The gathering continued on around us and Pikes started getting fed up with the lack of attention he was getting. He began to wander unsteadily about the place wearing nothing but a pink, see-through net petticoat with a beret and sunglasses. Yet still no one took any notice of him, particularly me, as I was busy. So he entered the room again, this time having ditched the skirt and he sat down in a chair. Unfortunately he now got even less reaction if that was possible, so he stood up, shouted that we were all boring bastards who were no fun at all and stormed out!

Although nothing much happened between Gaz and I it wasn't long before I began to moon over him. Wouldn't he have made a great boyfriend? Good looking and wild, with misspelt tattoos ('Ant Music for Sex Popple' anyone?) and always breaking into chemist shops. Sigh. How I romanticised them all.

> For you are wrong you guardians of our state
> You are misguided by your ignorance and hate
> These are angels; I am now amongst their kind
> Somehow they sparkle though so much maligned.
> And I have lived with rich man and with poor,
> Here at the bottom, is what I'm looking for.
> Never have I tasted so much tenderness and grace
> These are God's children; can you not see their face?

And they really were.

Birthday celebrations were not over yet though, because on the Saturday QOS held one of her famous 'Toga' parties. I wore an old peach satin sheet of mine that had come from the four-poster. Once there, I finally met up with the famous Tufty. He was cute in the extreme, with dark eyes and eyebrows, and he preferred his hair bleached white or vivid pink or green to match the two Day-Glo squids from the fishing tackle shop that he constantly wore on a plaited string around his neck. Then bloody Dennis took it upon himself to turn up, so I had a go at him and told him, 'to grow up', which was daring of me; then I stormed out into the kitchen to see Gaz, but he was having none of it either this time. During the course of the night some disreputable glue sniffers from the Hill gate crashed the place and nicked Leda's home-made leather jacket along with £60 from QOS's purse (such was the measure of our devotion, that we later had a collection for her). It broke up after that and we walked home to the sound of birdsong.

Gaz lived in a squat down by the dole office, so after that I was always having a nose in the window to see if I could spot him and Pinz would say that he was probably hiding from me, because they used to bump into him on the street all the time. But at least it took my mind off Peg Leg for a while. Then Dad sent Leda another letter telling her not to be a hooligan (?) and that it was such a shame about her hair. He added that he thought we were, 'Being kept happy on the dole'. 'Well I would be happy if I had more bloody money mate', I said.

As a result of the fact that all us work shy louts were constantly being rowdy round at her gaff, Mum's landlady began to get a bit fed up. Mum was thinking of getting out of there soon anyway, because she had got a tiny bit of money through at last from the sale of our lovely old house and we went to look at a tall terraced place that was up for sale in one of the county roads near Grandma's. A couple of teachers opened the door and during the course of our viewing they made it clear that they thought I was a nineteen year-old at college. In order to secure her mortgage at this time Mum had had to lie about her earnings and her age, so we had both 'clocked' (as they say in the motor trade) ourselves by five years.

Then our mate J.J. succumbed to the brain tumour that we had all pretended was not happening, Leda and I sent some flowers to his funeral and then we went and experienced the muted atmosphere in the pub for a while. We walked home down Vaughan Road in the rain and I espied a blond 'haircut' approaching on the opposite pavement. It was Gaz again at last.

'Hello' he shouted, 'Hello, how are you?'

'Okay, thanks' he answered and tripped over. But we all kept on walking.

> What whim of fate was it our feet
> Should at the same time walk the street?

And at that point our paths should cross,
For you a gain, for me a loss.
And how I wished that you might stray
From your dark path to my dark way

But that was not to be. As the summer progressed and it got hotter, I could on odd occasions, be seen doing normal things like baking cakes and pruning the roses. 'The Dynamic Duo' went off on holiday, so various mates came over to see me and I dyed their hair for them. Brian came over to jam with Leda and she was rapidly earning her place in local legend, striding about over Harrow Hill, dressed in ripped jeans and a top hat, with my dog alongside her. I accidentally got sunburnt, which wasn't very Goth. Talking of Goths, Flying Eyebrows had started to bring this new young guy out with her. He was tall, with long dyed black hair. He constantly wore a full-length black leather coat and his face was plastered in white make-up. 'Foundation Face' (as he quickly became known), was out going in the manner of Robert and I quite liked him, because at least he bothered to be flirty and to make an effort with me. We invited everyone back to Grandma's after the pub and Duncan who was drinking whilst on antibiotics, was sick in the garden (it took years for the grass to grow back on that patch). We watched 'The Rocky Horror Picture Show', but the beautiful limping Riff Raff only made me long for Peg Leg once more.

It was July 1985 and time for 'Live Aid', so we set off to a party that we'd heard about, and ended up being driven round Watford's one-way system about a million times before getting stopped by the pigs. The party, when we did get there, was far from lively itself unfortunately, but I met some different people; one of whom said,

'Hello sexy, I've only ever seen someone like you on a post card', before trying for ages to get off with me.

Oh no, Dennis was there as well, but he had decided to be half decent to me after my recent shouting at him. Pinz spent the evening snogging some creep on the stairs and the rest of us gathered round the TV set to watch the show. I felt slightly miffed as Eric played 'White Room' without the others, but I thought that Freddie Mercury was by far and away the best as he led the crowd in a rousing rendition of 'We Are The Champions.' Not very Punk was I? I even sang Saint Geldof's praises, so I must've been out of it. Seriously, in those naïve days we truly believed in it all. On the way home in the car, Pinz put her hand on Dennis's leg and I got annoyed but she twigged fairly quickly and was very sorry. We got dropped off at Mum's where I watched the rest of the show and swooned over Keith Richards. Now that is a geezer.

When I was living at North Avenue my greatest paranoid fear was that a burglar would climb up onto the conservatory roof and try to get in through the bedroom window, which was right next to my bed. One night, I was happily sending out the zeds when I became aware of a noise that sounded suspiciously like someone trying to gain entry. This was followed by a soft and insistent tapping at the pane and I nearly died of heart failure before Leda's voice said, 'Nettie, let me in, I've forgotten my key.' We then settled down to our nightly summer performance of the cat meowing to get in at the window and the dog panting to get out of the room.

Next up, Dad said he had some work in the U.S.A (he never let on to us at the time that this was to work with John Lydon in New York on the PiL album 'Rise') and wanted someone to go out to Italy and do the horses. Leda ended up going and she took a member of the hippy crew with her for company. So Leda and a hippy were out riding one fine day high up in the beautiful Tuscan hills, when suddenly the horses took fright and bolted, with the result that both riders (hippy man being a non-riding type) hit the deck. Hippy man said, 'Oh ouch' and went off to bed, leaving Leda the 'very 'ard indeed' to catch both nags, untack them, put them away and feed them, as she hopped about with a broken leg! She was then taken off to an out of the way non-English speaking Italian hospital, where she had to stay for a while until they let her come home.

Phil and I drove up to Gatwick Airport to meet her. The construction of the M25 motorway was well under way by then and it was ruthlessly carving its concrete path directly through the many quiet woods and bridleways that I had known so well in my Chalfont days. At the airport, we waited for Leda who appeared abruptly out of the customs hall, grinning under her ginger mohican, holding her crutches aloft and seated in a bleeping luggage cart driven by a burly member of the airport staff.

Back at base, the pub had suddenly become inundated with hoards of Spanish tourists, which prompted us to burst into a loud rendition of 'Viva Espana', much to our own amusement but not to theirs. Duncan then decided to have a pretend gay attack, and had dallied with the pretty Richard all night; I don't know what the outcome was, but they were last seen lying semi-conscious on the pavement. Further along, we encountered Phil hanging over the Roxborough Bridge declaring dramatically, 'I want to be alone' in his best Garbo impersonation, so we left him there and the sound of his cries receded into the darkness.

I had also managed to acquire another admirer who would often lay in wait for me along the streets. His usual *modus operandi* if he saw me approaching, was to hide in a telephone box until I got near enough and then to spring out as if by chance, in order to chat and walk along with me. This oft repeated scenario led to him becoming known as, 'Telephone Box Man' and he was a nice guy, but as usual not what I was after. Others were also pairing up; some country Punks from Ledbury came to visit us and Pinz took up with one who resembled Worzel Gummidge. QOS was getting it together with Bondy and in August I went with them and Seamus (who wasn't happy about this development), to the farewell GLC thing up on The South Bank, where we walked along and admired the London rooftops that stood out in dark relief against the sunset. A huge crowd had gathered around County Hall and we got hoisted up onto the roof of a coach to get a better view, which was a very painful experience I can tell you, but everybody cheered us. The show began in earnest and strange figures from a group calling themselves 'Urban Sax' (who were wearing space suits and playing saxophones), began abseiling down the building and sprayed foam over everyone as a finale. Telephone Box Man appeared from nowhere out of the crowd to say, 'Hi'.

Getting down again from our vantage point was another major hassle with Seamus and I both getting cut as a result of getting caught up in my rings. When I'd recovered sufficiently from the ordeal, we piled into the Embassy Club, which was full of posy Goths, where we danced the night away. I got really hot, my hair flopped and QOS had her handbag stolen, but then she found £11 on the floor so that made up for it. Eventually, we dawdled down Oxford Street and bought some food, then waited an hour for the 4.30 a.m night bus, which arrived back at Harrow Bus Station just as the rosy hues of a vivid pink dawn were spreading out across the sky. As I passed Mum's place Dennis leaned out of the window and beckoned me in there. So I went in for a short while and then Telephone Box Man, who just happened to be in there as well, elected to walk me home. Shame it wasn't anyone hunky.

I was still quite partial to the young tattooed Gaz actually, but I had noticed that he was hanging around a lot with the junkie contingent; and then the attractive 'H please Bob' appeared looking smacked out of his head and I could tell it a mile off. Yes, there was quite a bit of it about and the local TV news programme 'London Plus' identified our town as being 'The Drug Centre of North London,' where you could 'allegedly' buy wraps of heroin on the cheap in the Bus Station. Not that I ever came across any evidence of this whatsoever whilst waiting for a bus, but then again I do often tend to miss the obvious. It is true that a fair few souls got messed up, but others dabbled a bit and carried on to do fine in life without ever resorting to it again, so it is possible. But I could never be bothered to risk getting stuck in the boring, demanding and very often life-long commitment that drug addiction entails. Meanwhile, those of us who could still walk and talk with some degree of coherence (most of us in fact) continued to make the best of our lives unencumbered by the worry of where we were going to get our next fix and the stress of having to lie to every one about it.

Flying Eyebrows (who actually went by the name of a Fifties icon), always laboured under the misapprehension that she was incredibly a la mode, which never failed to amuse me, because in reality her name was Debbie and she came from Harlow. Nevertheless, she whisked me off with her one night to a party in Greenford she had been invited to and it was stuffed to the gills with 'Mud Club' trendies such as Dionne, who was a glamorous transwoman attired in a shimmering swimsuit and wearing huge stilettos. She towered over the ugliest man in the world, who in turn was dressed in a silver toga and had a large sequinned tiara on his dark head (this turned out to be the uber cool Phillip Salon). Next to him was a strange French bloke sporting a hat that looked like a flowerpot. I wasn't very enthused by that lot I can tell you, mainly because they were standing about doing precisely nothing. Look interesting by all means, but try and enjoy yourself whilst you're doing it. Thank goodness that there were also some yobbos who'd come up from Devon and they were really nice blokes. I got on quite well with them and had a good chat in the kitchen with a bloke who had an orange mohican and then another one came to find me and he offered me a smoke. Flying Eyebrows annoyed me on the way home by saying that Foundation Face was madly in love with her and wanted her to chuck Brian; because I thought that he had already been seriously chatting *me* up. I began to realise then that she did enjoy a bit of a fabrication.

'Is any of this true?' I asked myself.

She then announced that she wanted every girl in Harrow to be jealous of her, which I thought was an odd ambition. She felt that she was a serious contender for QOS's crown, but in that respect she was outclassed in every direction. Being a nicer person may have helped.

I was delighted to be able to let rip properly once more when a large group of us went off to a gig at 'Cedar's Youth Club', in Wealdstone. At least twenty-five Punks met up at the Bus Station and piled onto a 186. We walked down to Cedars through the park and paradoxically we felt united in our nonconformity. We got a kick out of the horrified glances that we attracted from the passers by and even a bedraggled mongrel trotting innocently along on the path in front of us took one look and then legged it! This gig was in aid of the Miner's Strike and had been organised by Tufty. Oh yes, we were about as 'right on' as it was possible to be in those days; throwing our weight behind organisations like, 'Rock Against Racism' and 'The Anti-Nazi League' as well as harbouring a passionate hatred towards all the NF skinheads. Tufty and his band played spirited renditions of The Pistol's 'Anarchy in the UK', Hawkwind's 'Silver Machine' and The Damned's version of 'Happy Talk'. We rucked and pogoed and barged each other about with gusto (apparently, this is now known as 'moshing'). In the spirit of our times we christened Tufty 'the Bob Geldof of Harrow' and after the gig we carried on partying at his latest squat in Wealdstone. Another girl whom I found irritating had also started hanging about with us all (and by that I mean that she was attractive and all the blokes were after her). Her name was Pauline and she was a grubby bleached blonde, who chewed gum all the time and spoke really common. Gaz was there and was surrounded by women who were far more attractive than I could ever hope to be, such as Yawn and Pauline. I realised then that he was one for the ladies and a bastard and how I bet he wishes he were back there right now.

Although I was unlucky with men, my female friendships continued to blossom. I still saw Jap from time to time and I would occasionally go up to her very smart town-house in Linton Street in Islington, where she and her husband Paul were still having a marvellous time. They had, with Ethel the Aardvark's help, restored this place from a bomb-damaged wreck. The area was up and coming and one of 'The Boomtown Rats' lived across the road. I attended a party there where a Yuppie accused me of being a 'Pinko' because I disagreed with Poppy's Dad for selling the 'Upside Down House' on Sudbury Court Drive (for which he'd been offered an extortionate amount to open the area up for new development in the Greenbelt). On the other hand, back in Punk world, QOS's mother startled me by saying that she thought I was a 'Fascist' because I mentioned that I'd long nurtured a secret desire to wave the union flag at the Last Night of the Proms and sing 'Land of Hope and Glory!' Fascist or Communist? Posh or Common? Make your bloody minds up!

QOS obviously felt that I wasn't too closely associated with The Gestapo at that time, because she took me out for a pizza one evening. Then we went off to The Roxborough to play Pool with the 'in' crowd. Tufty enjoyed a special place in this circle and he was there with his sixteen-year-old girlfriend Zazie. Later, when we were walking back round to QOS's for a cuppa, we encountered Pinz and Duncan on their way home from The Beard. They were severely messing about and amused me no end, but back at QOS's all the rest of the 'cools' once again expressed their disdain and disapproval of this slightly less 'with it' contingent. It wasn't class or age that set them apart, it was an obscure difference that they seemed to have invented and it was in some measure analogous to serious Bauhaus chic versus trivial End of the Pier slapstick. Is your make-up art or are you a clown? Punk U and non U. Whatever it was, I always found it ridiculous. Snobby socialists no less!

There was nothing wrong with my little bunch as far as I was concerned. I became their hairdresser now and would go round to Sharon's in South Harrow, to do everyone's sides with the clippers. Then Pinz, Big Lisa and several others would come round to me and I'd apply various shades of dye to whatever hair they had left. With our freshly coloured barnets lacquered up, we barged into The Roxborough one night to see a psychedelic Punk outfit called 'Rubella Ballet.' All the usual suspects were already in situ and were supplemented by many more from far and wide. There were orange, purple, pink, green, yellow, and blue mohicans and some of the highest hairstyles in the world, bigger than Pinz's even. It must've taken them hours. The band wore glowing fluorescent colours and the drummer was gorgeous. A six foot nine blond with wonderful eyes and high cheekbones; he looked just like 'Lurch' off 'The Munsters' TV show and I was dying to say, 'You rang?'

Peg Leg put in an appearance and QOS began telling me that I could get him really easily. Haven't we heard this somewhere before? Please tell me how exactly. Then Dennis turned up with Legs and they gave me a smoke and offered me some speed, which I declined. They wanted me to go off with them to a club. Dennis had by now had all his hair cut off and I thought he looked awful. After the gig, we all hung around outside and huddled under our umbrellas in the rain. Peg who had been there on his own and had been looking over at me all night, came up to say goodbye. Eventually we dispersed, feeling a bit disappointed that there were no parties on anywhere.

But we cheered up when Mum invited Pinz, Leda and I, to her double-glazing company's work 'Fun Day' in the Buckinghamshire village of Stoke Poges. Needless to say, we did get some stick because of our hair but Pinz and I struck up a rapport with an elderly gent in the beer tent and he thought we were so fantastic that he asked to have his photo taken with us. Pinz upset the kid's conjurer because she was so much funnier than he was and she took up with a little boy called Scot, with whom she proceeded to career about using Leda's crutches as machine guns and playing 'Rambo.' Two guys came up and gave us a smoke, whilst the dog played and swam, met new people and got fed with steak. We left at about 7:30pm, feeling so out of it that we had to keep our eyes shut in the car in order to avoid being sick. When I got in I had to revive my hair, which had flopped, have a cup of tea and some food and be ready for when Pinz knocked for me at nine. Foundation Face had telephoned me the previous day and said he'd be up the pub and lo and behold, he actually was. Everybody seemed to be having arguments though; so Marc and I sat together and said, 'Oh God, why do people have to be so heavy all the time?'

This was the big thing then. No one wanted any 'hassles' or 'heavy vibes'; what that meant was that they didn't want to be put on the spot or to be held accountable for anything. Nevertheless, Foundation Face was pleasantly light and flirty, but even then I noticed a flash of Robert in his eyes, which didn't bode well. He rang me the next day and said I should think of somewhere for us to go out, but I said I was too busy that week. Bloody hell! I felt too old for messing about, why didn't he think of somewhere to bloody go? He was too weedy for me I'm afraid and reminded me too much of Robert. I mean he'd never even tried to kiss me yet. How slow can you get? It was Bank Holiday Monday, we were all skint and Pinz was rather subdued in the pub that night as a result of having witnessed a bloke getting killed in a motorcycle accident outside her house. Then to cap it all, Pauline and her chewing gum came and joined us for a chat and I just knew that she was going to get in my way at some point.

Mum had decided to try and raise some cash by auctioning Dad's Perspex drum kit at Sotheby's. When it went in she got cross with Hilary Kay who said that in her opinion it wouldn't reach the reserve price, which (yah boo sucks) it did. In fact, it came on the radio and Grandma shouted down the stairs to me that the kit had fetched nearly £4,000. We were dancing about with joy at the prospect of this major injection of funds into our cash strapped lives. (Mum gave us £100 each for a shopping spree and put the rest towards furniture for our new house when we got it.)

I wished my good fortune would continue and that Peg would come round with a bunch of flowers and say, 'I love you;' but I realised that there was more hope of them raising the bloody Titanic than of that happening. And as they have since located the vessel and brought the stuff up and Peg never did love me, I feel that that was indeed an accurate prediction. Mind you, I couldn't blame him for not liking me, because Mum got some photos back that she'd taken of us all and I thought I looked disgusting, with a face like a fat bit of dough with currants for eyes.

The weather got very hot and that seemed to carry over onto us lot at the pub as tempers became frayed. Zola and a couple of other girls were fighting over Tim and then Bee and Flying Eyebrows got annoyed when Foundation Face bought me a drink. Pinz and I decided to leave them all as we'd heard about a nurse's party up at Northwick Park Hospital, so we took a few friends and headed off to find it. It was Tony Wormtongue who had told us about it and this should have alerted us to the fact that we were off on a wild goose chase, because we then wandered about all over the place, up and down stairs and in a lift for ages and ages. Luckily, the adventure in itself amused us greatly anyway, even if we never did find the party.

Hippy Trevor decided to get married to some beautiful but strange (as in 'I've been sectioned') girl he'd taken up with. We didn't particularly approve, but I went along to the party for it, which they held at Phil's place. I spent the afternoon dancing away to Billy Idol's 'White Wedding', 'which was fairly apt. Later on, Pinz and Tim found me sitting on the pavement at the end of Vaughan Road, drinking a can of Pils. Hic!

After the pub, we went back to the party, which was still going strong. Dennis became very attentive and amazingly he asked me to go home with him. I acquiesced mainly because I thought I should still feel something for him, but even as we drove off down towards Greenford I began to have my doubts. The familiar room reeked of stale beer and fags and looked as shabby and unkempt as its lonely occupant. I found it very hard to come to terms with the fact that I no longer had any passion left in my heart for him. I noticed that an unpleasant feeling of emptiness had crept in to replace it and for the first, but not the last time, I understood how an ageing and jaded roué must feel. We stood and kissed in the recess of the bay window and the voice of Stuart Adamson (who had once gyrated about on stage in Peterborough wearing his pink spandex cat suit) sang a pain filled refrain from the record deck on the shelving at the end of the bed.

> *'Oh Lord, where did the feeling go?*
> *Oh Lord, I've never felt so low.'*
> ('Chance': Big Country)

It couldn't have been more appropriate. Oh well, as I was there. I lifted up my arms and took my top off. 'You've got great tits.' 'I know.'

And that was our last time.

# CHAPTER SIX
## Outlaws

*'Be exactly who you want to be, do what you want to do*
*'cos he is he and I am me, but you're the only you.'*
(Crass)

E verything continued to get out of hand at an alarming rate and I was oblivious of all but the desire to look outrageous and find a man who was happy to do the same. My dear Peg Leg and his Gothic Alison kept breaking up and getting back together again. She often confided in me that her previous boyfriend, whom she still liked, was pressing for a reconciliation, but as I still loved old Peg I didn't feel I was in much of a position to offer her any advice. He liked her a lot I think because she was so beautiful and that seemed to be the main qualification that he required in a girlfriend, and why not? Had I been stunning I feel sure that he would have gone out with me and then I would have had plenty of time in which to become fed up to the back teeth with him.

Any road up chaps, just for a change there was a party. It was billed as a 'Pimps and Tarts', as if we needed any excuse. I wore stockings and suspenders for the first time and finally came to understand their importance in the female armoury. It is true that Peg Leg had been watching me and hanging around a bit on the occasions when his girlie wasn't with him and she wasn't with him at this party either. So I made a serious play for him, which ended up with us having 'passionate' (I find this hard to believe now) sex on Grandma's living room floor. He did tell me that he found me 'sexually attractive' (what an honour!) and said that he couldn't keep saying 'no' to me (!), but that we must just stay friends and not do it again whilst he was still with her and not tell anyone and guilt, guilt, guilt. This does get very tiresome with men.

I encountered beautiful Gothic Alison the next day when the band 'Conflict' played down at The Roxborough. As usual, the place was packed with haircuts and the Police sent three vans along, in anticipation of mega-trouble from us scary looking lot and of course there wasn't any. Alison was as friendly as ever and I told myself that I didn't feel guilty, as it was no big deal. I spoke to her again at a party that Bee and Tris held at a flat they were renting together down in Wealdstone and it was there that I noticed a tall guy with spidery limbs, spiky dark hair and an interestingly pointed face. He had come up from the wilds of Peckham in South London and he was closely affiliated to a band called Night Music that Big Tris played the drums in. He was definitely attractive in a dangerous sort of a way and although I didn't even speak to him that night, I filed his face away in my memory before I got back to agonising about bloody old Peg.

A few nights later, the phone rang and when Grandma answered I heard a deep male voice ask for me, but when I said 'hello' he put the phone down and I felt sure that it was Peg having some sort of nervy b. His birthday fell in October and so I decided to splash out cash I could ill afford on a present. I'm certainly not above attempting to buy the affections of those I covet, so I bought him a large, black umbrella with a wooden handle and I wrapped it flamboyantly. He arrived at the pub feeling low because Alison had not appeared, so poor Peg had to make do with me as the booby prize. After a boozy evening, he kissed me and said he was too drunk to make it home so I asked him to come back to mine. Unfortunately, my master plan was completely foiled when when a new friend we knew as 'blonde Lisa' offered him a lift to Rayners Lane and I could cheerfully have throttled her.

When we arrived at Drake Court he was so out of it that I had to help him out of the car and he lurched off into the darkness with his pockets stuffed with wrapping paper and trailing long strings of ribbon behind him.

I forgot my angst for a while though, because we were about to move into our new house and be reunited as a dysfunctional family once more. Yes, we had finally acquired the place in Somerset Road. Contracts had been exchanged and we planned to hold a massive moving in party on 15th November 1985. Invitations had already gone out stating 'Mad Max & Rocky Horror fancy dress please'; though we were unprepared for the panic stations caused by the fact that we only got hold of the keys at three o'clock on that very same afternoon. The light had faded into a chill autumnal dusk as we set up a tape player for the music and erected a trestle table for the dips, crisps and booze. We put red bulbs in all the rooms and then turned the lights on in the empty house. As night fell, our new home became packed out with Goths, Punks and Hippies who cavorted about in outfits of every description. Legs and Shuggy, who were dressed in matching white boiler suits, acted as our bouncers and they wisely exercised their discretion by letting in those gatecrashers who were suitably attired in stockings and suspenders. A Hell's Angel called something like 'Goat', thought he was well 'ard and got into a row with Leda over the music. He boasted that he was going to call up the Los Angeles chapter to come and kill us, but Shuggy intervened by calmly handing him the telephone and saying, 'Be my guest.' Then Legs appeared behind him through the kitchen door and that was the end of that.

In the dining room, various freaks danced about to my homemade tapes of Rocky Horror songs, 'The Monster Mash' and a varied selection that included The Clash, The Sex Pistols, Generation X, Siouxsie and the Banshees, Crass, The Buzzcocks, Sham 69, Lou Reed, Adam Ant, Billy Idol, David Bowie, Echo and the Bunnymen, Talking Heads, Tears for Fears, music from The Blue's Brothers' and God knows what else. QOS sat on the front room carpet, wearing a red bra, matching briefs with suspenders and black stockings. She was chatting to Yawn who nodded her heavily lacquered black hair and fluttered her false eyelashes. Gothic Alison reclined in the corner looking as beautiful as ever with her pretty face and with her endless legs stretched out before her. She looked happy to be back with this guy of hers who happened to be a guitarist in that Night Music band from Peckham. (How much I envied her and I needn't have done, because she passed away from the big C, still a young girl, quite some time ago.)

Under the window lolled Adam and Zola, who were now an item. He was clad in leather and weighted down with chains, whilst her orange hair was spiked up high. No hair however could hope to out do the enormous construction that Pinz exhibited. I wore a long black T-shirt, the inevitable stockings and suspenders (now that I'd discovered their worth) and had a spider web drawn across the side of my head. The Bell turned up, but was well out of his depth. Hippy Phil wore animal prints and looked like he'd just come out of the jungle! I noticed that the lanky and edgy thing from Bee and Tris's party had also put in an appearance *sans* invitation. He did look good all dressed in black and he had a great voice coupled with a cheeky, intelligent personality. He had been sitting on the floor in the hall for some time skinning up with my sister. I was standing by the stairs when he suddenly appeared in front of me, grasped the banisters on either side, so that I was trapped and said, 'I think you're really beautiful'.

I didn't need any persuading whatsoever at all to spend the rest of the night tangled up with this vision, who was universally known as 'Mad'. Peg Leg stared at me in sad disbelief as I rapidly forgot all about his existence on the planet. Mad and I retired to the bathroom and christened the house (start as you mean to go on), whilst people rattled the door handle and shouted, What's going on in there?' through the keyhole.

In the morning, Mad came up the road to Grandma's with me to get some breakfast. I took my make-up off and I was sure that he was thinking, God, I must have been drunk last night,' as I walked him up to the Roxborough Bridge to get the train. However, he did say, 'Look, whatever happens I promise I'll come back and see you again' And I thought, 'Yeah, yeah I bet.'

Soon enough, all the furniture arrived from the warehouse and had to squash itself into its considerably smaller surroundings. The dining room was filled from floor to ceiling with packing cases that took ages to sort through and they seemed mainly to be filled with hundreds of out of date bottles of bitter lemon that had for some reason accumulated in the old walk in larder. The previous occupants had left the front room curtains in situ and they were fashioned from a ghastly striped yellow satin. My mother said in true Oscar Wilde style that they 'really did have to go,' but Duncan however, became quite enamoured of these gaudy drapes and expressed his desire to have them made up into an extravagant seventeenth-century pirate's outfit. He then said he would add an eye patch, a tri-corn hat and have a parrot upon his shoulder. Thus attired he planned to play the accordion and sing *'what shall we do with the drunken sailor?'* very loudly, whilst riding a unicycle along the pedestrian tunnels of the tube network. This was an amusing thought to hold onto as I took the train up to The Moscow Arms with Zola, Adam, Slimy, Peg and a bloke called Adrian. On the way back, we stopped on the rainy windswept Marylebone Road and I used one of those new fangled, heated, musical toilets for the first time and wondered what they would think of next? Peg was looking at me again all the way back on the train and the next night he came back to mine after the pub where he remained when everyone else had gone home. He sat there looking like a solemn hornpiece and I wondered what he thought was going to happen? In a bed at last, but he had another neurotic attack afterwards because he thought I was going to get the wrong idea again. How boring this can be and he wasn't a patch on Mad anyway. 'You've saved my life tonight' he said as I piled him into a taxi at six o clock in the morning but I wasn't that desperate anyway because Foundation Face was always ringing me up and girly Richard from the Edgware parties wrote me a letter.

At the same time, Big Lisa had started a romance with a girl whose boyfriend was getting in the way, so they sort of dumped him on us and then Pinz ended up with him. He was an awful, Irish, alcoholic and argumentative man called Gerry and he tagged along with us to see a band called The Fits who were playing at The Roxborough. The highlight of my evening came when the lead singer asked me to help him with his hair after I bumped into him doing his make-up in the girl's toilets. However, things went downhill when the stroppy bar stuff pulled all the plugs at eleven and the band got the hump. Consequently, stupid drunken Gerry saw some aggro and started having a tussle with the band without having the faintest idea what he was fighting about. Leda stormed in and sorted it all out thank goodness. At the end, I approached the singer and said, 'Thank you very much, I enjoyed myself.'

'Come and see us in London next time, its safer,' came his exasperated reply.

When Leda and I got home and were getting ready for bed, we became aware of a loud banging going on, followed by the sound of stones being thrown at Leda's bedroom window from the street. Who the bloody hell can that be at two o'clock in the morning? We opened the front door only to be confronted by Dennis all on his own and swaying about on the doorstep in the frosty night. Long gone were the days when I thought, 'Oh I love him so' in fact now I felt like saying, 'Oh no, please fuck off!'

But we let him in and sat about in our nighties for a while whilst he rolled us a couple of joints and we got a bit stoned. I'd never even been his friend and I felt I had nothing whatsoever to say to him so I wasn't very polite and gave him the hint to leave, which he took and went storming off into the night, slamming the door behind him. Yes, the scales had fallen from my eyes and I recognised him as the seedy old drunkard that he was and always had been. Still, it just goes to show how much they love you once you hate them.

And Peg who was heading in the very same direction, upset me yet again on another trip up to The Moscow Arms. He kept moaning on to me about how much he wanted to find a girl to chat up, which I thought was bloody charming. I proceeded to get very drunk and on the way home I behaved very naughtily on the station platform, by taking all the litter out of the bin and throwing it on the rails in an incredibly puerile act of vandalism for which Adam quite sensibly told me off.

Once on the train, several of us burst into a loud

rendition of 'Molly Malone', which I'm sure was music to the ears of all the other late night passengers. The last trains sometimes stopped at Neasden then, so I took that opportunity to get off and go for a wee and my brother Kofi decided it would be a good idea to accompany me. Unfortunately, the very last train of the night arrived on the opposite platform to where we were and so we had to run for it. On ahead sprinted my lithe young sibling and he raced down the steps to hold open the door of the waiting train. As I careened at full pelt, with my metal spiked heels ringing on the concrete, I failed to notice an ankle height bar in the corridor at the top of the steps. This was in place prior to the station staff pulling the iron gate across and locking up for the night. I hit this bar at speed and went crashing to the ground. There was no time to stop, so I was up immediately, hobbling along as fast as I could with my stockings all ripped and I just got on to the train before the doors slid shut. All eyes were on me and oh dear, I had really hurt myself.

'Have I annoyed you?' enquired Peg Leg's voice down the telephone wire the next day. Amazingly, he had managed to work it out for himself, but what his motives were I never did know. Flying Eyebrows however, usually made her motives very clear and she knew Mad and 'The Night Music' crew. Although I wasn't vastly enamoured with the idea of her being directly involved in my romantic life, for the time being she gave the appearance of furthering my suit by informing me that Mad had sent me his 'best regards.' She said that he had asked her for my phone number but that unfortunately she had not been in possession of it at the time (we believe you). She added that maybe we should both go and stay over in Peckham sometime because the lead singer loved her so much. That sounded marvellous to me but I hadn't yet realised that of course a guy as lovely as Mr Mad already had a very nice girlfriend thank you, down in his own neck of the woods.

Talking of woods and countryside bits, I went down to be even more 'right on' man and hang out with the ladies of Greenham Common. Actually, it was an informative day out spent with QOS, her mother, Big Lisa and Solo the dog (who really did have a marking like a peace sign upon his head). Lisa and I had a laugh about her awful garlic sandwiches. Then she pointed the metal three pronged picnic stool at me and sang, *'Nettie Baker, its all over, your mission is a failure, your lifestyle's too extreme,'* in the voice of Riff Raff from The Rocky Horror Show.

(It was Lisa who first used the phrase 'The Barmy Bakers' to describe our family. She had a massive crush on the actress Jill Gascoine from 'The Gentle Touch' TV series and she also had one on my Mum. This resulted in her oft-used phrase, 'Your Mother's a wonderful woman.')

It was grey and cold that day at Greenham and the rags and ribbons tied onto the chain link fencing blew about in the winter wind, as the high keening sounds made by the women carried away into the dull and empty sky. Police horses barged along through massed ranks staging a sit down and I felt very sorry for the poor nags who were desperately trying not to tread on anyone and simultaneously I felt very cross with the police for forcing them to do so.

I got home that evening feeling well knackered but I had already arranged to go with Flying Eyebrows for a night out at the highly 'Gothic' Kit Kat Club. I listlessly dragged on a completely see-through antique black lace dress (given to me by QOS), but I hung about feeling tired still, so I asked my Mother if perchance she had any 'wake up drugs'. She handed me a wrap of Amphetamine Sulphate, so I put some in a bit of fag paper, twisted it up, swallowed it and whoopi do, what a bloody marvellous job that did! Throughout the night, Flying Eyebrows effortlessly demonstrated her supremacy over me by getting off with a Goth. Then in the early hours she drove home with a triumphant smirk playing about her mouth and her red lipstick smudged all over her face. You may wonder why I bothered with her at all really, but don't forget her skills in the hairdressing department and the fact that she was also quite often in contact with Mad.

And one morning soon after, a Christmas card that bore a Peckham postmark, flopped down upon the mat. I tore it open and read, *'Sorry I didn't write earlier – trouble getting your address* [we know why!] *Please write and let me know of any House Wrecking parties over X-MAS. I'd be only too glad to bring my chainsaw. My address is on the back of this card, so you've got no excuse for not writing to me. May Santa bring you what you want and loads of Drugs to enjoy it with. I'm hoping he'll send me a Rubber Vicar outfit.*

*How's the Four Poster?*

*P.S. sorry about the cheap card, but I'm skint.*

*Merry\* Christmas*

*\*Merry – N. To be under the influence of any combination of Alcohol, Drugs and Cigarettes, usually leading to great amounts of time in the toilet emptying both ends.*

*Luv Mad xx*

I wrote straight back of course, but no, I didn't see him over Christmas. I had to be content with attending the 'Fuck Christmas' gig that Tufty had organised for us downstairs at The Roxborough.

My birthday arrived and Peg upset me in the pub as was his wont and afterwards, back at mine just to spite myself, I was sick and got off with Tim (or got off with Tim and was sick?). But On Christmas Eve however, the other correspondent in my life put in an appearance. Remember that girly Richard from the Edgware parties? No? I'd all but forgotten him myself by this time I have to admit. Anyway, he called me up and said he was in the area and wanted to meet up that very night. I acquiesced with some reluctance because I hadn't seen him since the previous February when I wasn't that weird looking and when he knocked on the door he appeared rather straight in comparison. But the main problem for me was his personality (his what?), which appeared to be irritating and dominant, so that inevitably a real battle of wills soon ensued. At the pub, one of his mates that I knew quite well turned up with a real horror show of a bird and he wanted us to go to another pub with them.

'Look mate, you go if you like' said I, 'but I've already arranged my Christmas Eve and I'm not moving anywhere, I want to be with my friends.' 'You can see your friends any time.' 'But I want to see them now!'

As a result of this, he elected to stay in the pub with me and I bet he wished he hadn't. He was all over me, which I quite enjoyed at first but it soon began to drive me round the bend; and I had to buy all his drinks! Then he was after all the girls and really reckoned himself, talking to everyone as though he'd known them for ages. In fact, he was so exactly like Robert that I felt sick! (Even though this is what had attracted me in the first place.) Anyway, we came back to my house (he'd arranged to stay the night, groan).

Of course we did do it (it being Christmas Eve), but it was a bit of a long effort if you get me. Then Christmas morning was upon us and I sat there ignoring him and opening all my lovely presents and he didn't have any. Ha, ha, it was funny. I mean you just don't get yourself into situations like that do you? Maybe it taught him a lesson, I do hope so. I just got up and began to get ready to meet

Pinz at the pub, then Richard's mate arrived to take him away and I thought, 'Hooray, I shall never have to see him again.' And I didn't.

I was pretty certain that he was bi-sexual, which was fine, but I didn't want AIDS thanks very much. We were only just becoming aware of the disease and I have to admit that no one ever did use a condom that I noticed. (Every single one of the people I knew that later got the disease was a heterosexual intravenous drug user.)

Later on, after a noisy dinner in our new dining room (looking exactly like the previous one only less than half the size), Dad phoned up and was most bemused to encounter a whole house full of noisy maniacs on the other end of the line. For without the restraints imposed upon us by incurring his displeasure, we had gone completely off the rails. On Christmas night, hoards of Punks descended on us for a visit because this was a haven where they could behave normally (meaning skin-up), away from parental restrictions. (Nevertheless, old Stripey Jayne's father must've been fairly okay, because he produced a series of festive photos, which featured some toy robins getting drunk on miniature bottles of Scotch at a birdbath. As the pictorial tale progressed, the birds got increasingly more inebriated, until they were lying on their backs with their legs in the air, wearing party hats and smoking cigarettes!)

On New Years Eve, I began the celebrations by bothering Peg, who ran away a lot, whilst little Zola messed about by trying to snog all the girls. Then as the bells rang the New Year in, Foundation Face appeared at my elbow and gave me a big French kiss. Then we all went off to a party at Phil's place where I saw all the old hippy lot, including Dennis who kept saying, 'Do you remember last year?' etc, etc, oh shut up Dennis! I just laughed and kissed Foundation Face right under his nose and then I took said Goth back to my house for some nook. Now I know very well that 'one man's meat is another man's poison', so I won't make any unkind comments about his size or performance; and truly for the time being I was thrilled to have a devoted and fairly good looking admirer in my bed. Soon after though, I began to think, 'Help, I'm not sure,' but felt I ought to persevere just for the kudos of actually having a boyfriend again at long last. We started seeing each other a bit, but then one Saturday morning another small brown envelope from Peckham flew through the letterbox and landed on the doormat.

*'Dear Nettie,* [It said,]

*Hope you had a good New Year. I did apart from some cunt punching a hole in my mouth. 4 fuckin' stitches – great start to the New Year. Make mine a double!!*

*Anyway, that's the griping out of the way. Would love to join you for several large ones some time. You name the time and place and I'll see if I've got any money.*

*I'm writing this at work* [the DHSS], *pretty trendy notepaper huh? Government issue no less! No expense spared. First day back and God I'm bored.*

*Seem to remember that you've got a bath, I think I'm going to have to come and use it sometime as we've got no hot water in ours.*

*Hope the four-poster is still okay. I enclose card just in case.*

[Enclosed card reads]

<u>Mr Mad</u>
<u>Four Poster Bed Inspection Services</u>
*\*Springs tested*
*\*Sheets soiled*
*\*Complete 'on the spot' bedding re-arranging*
*\*Swedish full body massage (sorry wrong card)*

*Went back home for X-MAS hoping to pick up loads of money and presents. Came back with a £1.50 Boots Gift Voucher and a stinking hangover. Did manage to contact some old acquaintances and it seems possible there could be some House Wrecking in Surrey later this year so get your sledgehammer packed. Might be in Scotland next month so I'll send you a post card.*

*Ooopss manager's just returned so I'll have to shoot off. See you soon, keep smoking, give the dog a kiss from me.*

*Lots a luv*
*MAD XXX*
*P.S Tell the dog to give you a kiss from me too.*
*Pass the RSPCA*
*P.P.S HAPPY NEW ONE!!*

Meanwhile, Foundation Face continued to pop round on a regular basis, but he shaved his armpits and his chest hair and the whole lot together put me in mind of a large lump of white dough. Anyway, there we were on the bed one day, when the phone rang and it was Mad. He said he was planning to come and stay in a couple of weekend's time, so I decided to tell Foundation Face to see what he would say. He said that he could handle it and went on to ask if he could stay the next night. Whilst I should I suppose have felt, 'Tally ho! The more the merrier', the boringly normal part of my soul just knew that it wasn't right.

Still, only two weeks and I might see Mad! But I had to be careful because Flying Eyebrows hadn't yet twigged that I was seeing Foundation Face and I didn't want her blabbing it about over Peckham way and ruining my chances. Pinz had also started seeing a very Gothic friend of Foundation Face's that we called 'Philbert the Frog'. I don't think that she was all that keen on him either because we often amused ourselves by singing a disparaging song about the poor bloke, that began *'Philbert the frog, sat on a log...'* Yes I rapidly went off Foundation Face in a big way and I began to agonise about it, because I felt mean. There was a 'Night Music' gig coming up at The Clarendon Ballroom in Hammersmith and I was desperate to go because I knew that Mad would be there. One night in the pub, Big Tris came up to me and said, 'Can I have a word in private?' as he dragged me to one side, 'There's a certain bloke who really wants to see you again called Mad,' he continued, 'do you want to see him again?'

'Er, I don't know, I suppose so.' He handed me a flyer for the gig and said that Mad would be there.

'But I'm seeing someone else,' I said.

'Well he can fuck off! On second thoughts bring him, it's another £1.50!'

This was typical of his humour and we both laughed.

I told Foundation Face that Mad would be at the gig and he said he'd 'try and be alright about it.'

But before we even got to the Clarendon, we were all off to a random gig by Tufty and Seamus in their respective bands, at a place called 'The People's Hall' in Shepherds Bush. This was a large, drafty and empty Victorian building, with several flights of stairs and corridors leading to huge open rooms that were freezing cold. As this was being organised by the 'Squat' lot and affiliated to the in-est of the 'In Crowd' it soon got very hostile and cliquey and Peg Leg was so pleased to see me when I arrived (without Foundation Face), that he rushed over to my side. Tufty, Nig and Pete entertained us quite well, but it really was too cold and groups of dishevelled and disgruntled Punks lurked around the walls, swigging Cider and Thunderbird wine, stamping their feet to keep warm and blowing fag smoke and steamy breath out into the vast, echoing spaces. Seamus was desperately trying to get everyone to stay and watch his band but I said, 'Bugger that!'

I wasn't best pleased because Peg had, in his inimitable style, already swanned off with two young ladies, so I got a lift back with Blonde Lisa. The next night, we went to see my brother's terrible Heavy Metal band play at 'Dingwall's' in Camden Lock. We'd got free tickets, so I took Duncan, Blonde Lisa and Foundation Face with me. The latter was too scared to brave the Gent's loos in all his make-up so he came into the Ladies with me. Kofi wasn't happy because they wouldn't allow him to use his own drum kit, then the one he did use generally fell apart whilst he played.

After two fairly naff evenings I was hoping that Hammersmith would be an improvement and it was. Foundation Face had appeared that afternoon being very devoted and we went up to West Harrow Station where we met up with Blonde Lisa, Tim and Matt, then onto to Rayners Lane where we collected Pinz, Sharon and another couple that we knew. We got to Hammersmith and settled in at a cosy corner of the bar, feeling rather jolly.

The Clarendon Ballroom in '86 was a bit of a wreck, but I'm sure that in the preceding decades it had been well sprauncey. A vast pale building with a large square frontage, it squatted on the roundabout just by the station where the (zzzz) shopping mall is now. At street level you entered a comfortable semi-circular bar that had a patterned carpet and alcoves of seats and tables along the opposite wall that made it seem snug and private. Above these recesses were Toulouse Lautrec prints of Can Can dancers at The Moulin Rouge. Upstairs boasted a large ballroom where bigger name bands would play and downstairs there was a smaller venue for the likes of our hopeful little combos. Sharon and Foundation Face had their backs to the door as I talked merrily to them and presently I noticed a tall, gangly thing with his hair much longer now and bleached blond, come loping through the entrance straight towards me. It had been well over two months since I'd seen him and he looked more gorgeous than ever. 'Hello,' said Mad.

The whole table went silent, whilst I had a minor heart failure and looked up at him all gooey eyed. After a brief chat, he went off; but in that time I had immediately compared him to Foundation Face and there are no prizes for guessing who came off worse. I began to make good headway getting drunk, whilst Mad lolled about at the bar with some other mates and my friends lost no time in telling me that he was extremely sexy indeed, as if I hadn't already noticed. We traipsed downstairs to see the band, which were better than I remembered; probably because I was more out of it this time than on the previous occasion that I'd seen them (I have some tapes still and let me tell you, they were diabolical). Nevertheless, Tris looked rather good hammering away on his drums wearing black eyeliner and flashing the tattoos on his well-muscled arms (more about that later).

Flying Eyebrows appeared with a mate of hers called Georgette whom I thought looked like a Muppet and was a right bitch. Not that you'd expect any less from an acquaintance of hers really. Well Eyebrows finally twigged about Foundation and she was not amused, but honestly I would've been more than glad for her to take him away when Mad came up to me again and said, 'I really will come and see you, but I've had so many problems, etc, etc,' Yeah, yeah, with your girlfriend you mean matey. Does he think I was born yesterday or what? But I was still starry eyed. Peg Leg was also there looking mean and moody. He got drunk and sat alone in a corner 'til I asked him to join us again upstairs and then he sat and regaled me with all his problems as usual. Later on, Foundation Face started hassling me to go home. God, I couldn't stand it. I said I just needed to pop down to the loo (because I'd seen Mad heading in that direction) and sure to brilliant plan, I met him coming up the stairs carrying two of Tris's drums. He said, 'Hello again' and kissed me. Swoon.

Then he repeated his previous conversation and then I kissed him and he said that he'd write. I thought perhaps he was just being nice to shut me up, but whatever it was, who cares? It made me realise what sort of man I did want. Then I passed Pinz entangled with some blonde mohican on the steps. On Philbert's night off as well!

After all that, we got ourselves in order to go home and we were all trashed except Foundation Face. Sharon had gone off to stay with some guy she knew, so it was Pinz, Blonde Lisa, Nikki, Peg, Matt, Tim and I on the train back. They all wanted to get on a train for Acton Town but Peg didn't want to because he said they'd still have to wait there for our train anyway. So Foundation and I waited with him. We three sat in the waiting room, with Peg and I sitting together chatting and Foundation Face seated opposite us reading a fanzine. When we got on the train, Peg asked me if I'd dye his hair red for him one day soon and I was delighted at the prospect of being stuck in the bathroom with him for a couple of hours. Sure enough, at Acton Town we were reunited with the rest of our gang who piled noisily back into our carriage. At Rayners Lane, Peg and Nikki waited with us for our connection and Peg said he wanted to come over and watch some Star Trek films. Goodness, what had come over him? I still didn't

The Whistling Waterfall, mid seventies. It lit the garden bright as day!

Camel Skull from the Sahara.

Oscar in the back garden.

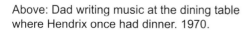

Above: Dad writing music at the dining table where Hendrix once had dinner. 1970.

Right (top): Mum outside our lovely house.

Right (bottom): Rock kids. Siblings Kofi & Leda, with gold discs, early 70s.

# Ordered out—and furniture goes too

SOLO the dog watches as furniture is removed. Ginger Baker's daughter Nettie, 24, and Paul Inder, 17-year-old son of Lemmy from Motorhead, stand on the pavement with their possessions.

THE EX-WIFE of rock drummer Ginger Baker was evicted last week from her home in Sudbury for a second time.

Liz Baker watched helplessly as furniture was removed from the £100,000-plus de-

tached house in Littleton Road.

Police officers stopped her going in as men from the sheriff's department entered the house on Thursday morning.

The eviction was the result of legal and fi-

nancial problems involving Ginger Baker, 45, who now lives in Italy.

**For storage**

Mrs Baker was ordered out of the house along with her eldest daughter Nettie, 24,

and a family friend, Paul Inder, 17, whose father is Lemmy of the heavy metal rock group Motorhead.

Furniture was taken away in a removal van for storage. On Thursday afternoon Mrs Baker said she planned

to stay with an uncle in Kingsbury for at least a few days.

Liz was evicted from her home a few months ago but her furniture was not touched and the family managed to get back in again.

Above: Eviction Day.
Solo, me & Lemmy's son Paul.
February 1985.

The Dynamic Duo, 14 North Avenue, mid 70s

Me and Leda in our
grandparent's back garden.

Robert returns:
Solo, Jo, Bill, me & Robert, 1985.

Outside the Royal Beard (Oak).
Stripey only got me to turn
round by asking Peg to say my
name! 1985.

Left: The Wasteland. Harrow squats.
Nig, Tufty & Hig.

Me in the kitchen, house warming,
November 1985.

Me & Sharon inside the 'Beard'. 1985.

Me, old boy & Pinz on the
Stokenchurch day out, 1985.

Leda & Mad.

A gaggle of Goths.

The famous curtains.

Gary.

Mad & me!

"Over sexed people" says the card!
Leda's birthday, February 1986.
Audrey, 'Big' Lisa, QOS,
Terry, Janet 'blue hair'.

Poster from Greenham common.

Tris.

Ian as a pirate.

Above: Jonah's 21st! Summer '86.
'Blonde' Lisa, me & Pinz.

Below: Bondy & QOS.

Tris.

Me, 1986
(*photo by Gaz Sherwood*)

Pinz & Tufty.

With my mate Duncan, 1986.

Leda Baker & Zillah Minx, Rubella Ballet, 1986.

Saddlewhores at The Clarendon, don't be late.

In the pub. Big fish, small pond & happy!

SADDLE WHORES

AT THE CLARENDON BASEMENT ON FRIDAY NOVEMBER 28th BE THERE EARLY

TOGA! Speeding in mauve lurex, June 1986.

Putney party. My nose & Tris with the knife. December '86.

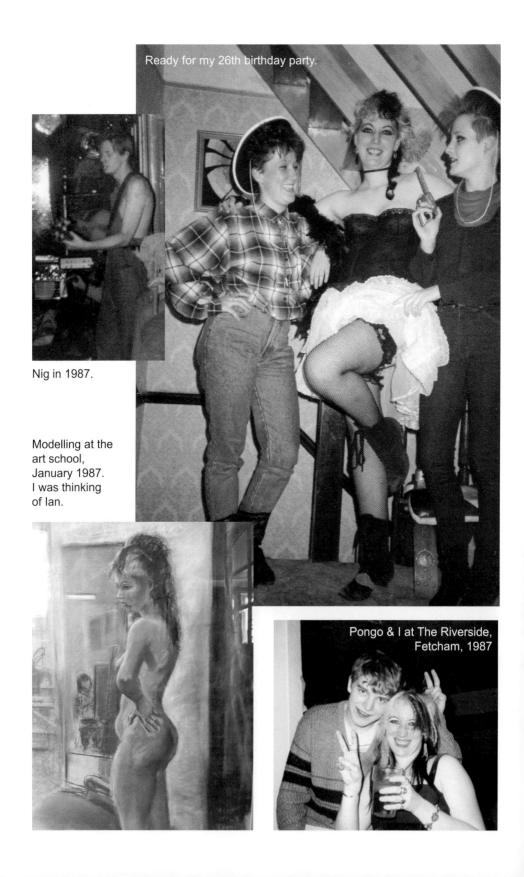

Ready for my 26th birthday party.

Nig in 1987.

Modelling at the
art school,
January 1987.
I was thinking
of Ian.

Pongo & I at The Riverside,
Fetcham, 1987

think it meant anything. Then he got cross at some normal folks in the waiting room when they called him a 'freak'. When we got in I felt terribly drunk, sick and emotionally confused, poor thing, and then Foundation had a rant about Mad and said he didn't want me to see him. Some hope of that. I slept badly due to alcoholic illness and Foundation snoring and taking up space etc. Now I'd decided that he reminded me of The Bell. The next day I went out and he stayed in my bed again for ages. Oh, please NO.

Pinz, Zola and myself all felt that we weren't happy with the men folk that we had so recently acquired and spent several hours discussing ways to rid ourselves of our unwelcome encumbrances without being too mean. Not that they however, gave a shit when the boot was on the other foot, but that is by the by. That evening Peg came over and said, 'You're looking very gloomy tonight, what's wrong?' and I have to say I was amazed that he'd noticed. I filled him in and he said basically, 'Just do it' and so I did. I dumped Foundation in a kind and caring manner (as if there is such a thing). But I did feel awful about it and as I left the pub, I said to Peg, 'I bet a huge lightning bolt strikes me dead as I walk out of here.' He smiled, 'Nah, it's never happened to me!'

I went home and dreamt that I met a Goth wearing a dark green frock coat and I hoped that it might be a premonition. The attraction of all these girly guys though had started to wear a bit thin. I needed somebody vulnerable yet strong, someone a bit macho. I was tired of poncy face paint and weediness. Mad was dithering about, he did ring up again and say, 'I haven't forgotten' etc, but I just knew that he was too lovely for the likes of me. I was still convinced that love must be out there and so I went on to do something else that was incredibly silly indeed.

# CHAPTER SEVEN
## 'Where's Captain Kirk?': 1986

*'The language of love slipped from my lover's tongue*
*cooler than ice-cream and warmer than the sun.'*
('Who's That Girl?', Eurythmics.)

O ver time, The Royal Beard public house had begun to fill up with ever more strange looking types who crossed our portals seeking respite from the derogatory remarks of the Beer Boys, Casuals, and Wedgies that hung about in the other watering holes around Harrow. Two girls who looked like they had walked out of an Edwardian fashion plate, in their high-necked, frilled blouses and hobble skirts, suddenly appeared one day and there was Vanessa, Slimy's new girl, who dressed just like a 'Cabbage Patch' doll. Another girl on the scene was a statuesque blonde who was known as 'Horsey Helen' (I presume because she wore long leather boots). Then there were the various colourful siblings and mates of all and sundry packed into our tiny end of the bar, adding to the buzz of a Friday and Saturday or the slightly less crowded hilarity of a week night.

Snow had fallen, settled and then frozen and the pavements were treacherous with ice. Peg had been round to see me and we'd had snowball fights as I walked him back to the station. Then On Friday, February 7th 1986, I went off to The Royal Beard as usual with Pinz, Tim and Zola. Big Tris was in there making his presence felt and at six foot two with his countless tattoos and a large black mohican that wasn't hard to do. I leaned over to Pinz and whispered, 'Don't tell anyone, but I really fancy him.' Afterwards, there was of course a party and it was just around the corner at a shared house in Springfield Road. Foundation Face followed me there and hung about with pain filled eyes, so I kissed him a bit, which of course gave him the wrong idea because then he thought he was going to stay at my house. Honestly, I was by this time behaving no better than everybody else, even though I thought different. Tris stood opposite me in the dark recess by the kitchen door. In his leather and studs, with his broad physique, he gave off a macho, protective, vibe. He had in fact, come along in the hope of scoring with Horsey Helen, but I went and chatted him up instead. He towered over me and I was immediately assailed with the scent of his 'Azzaro' aftershave. 'Where's Bee?' I asked, 'I've sent her home,' he said.

Eventually and without too much persuasion I got off with him. Foundation went off home and I didn't even notice, then Peg had a wiggy and gave me a long lecture about Bee but I wasn't listening and they can say 'no' can't they? Then he went and got into a fight about some girlie and I couldn't have cared less. Although I was feeling a bit sick after drinking vast quantities of red wine on top of three pints of Holsten. It was 5 a.m. when Tris, Philbert and I walked down the frozen wasteland of the Pinner Road to my place. Tris was so busy swearing Philbert to secrecy that he fell over on the ice, and we all laughed. So Philbert slept downstairs (I presume because he couldn't get home) and Tris slept with me. This was not a great thing to do to Bee though, but never mind, the deed was done and I was well aware that I would have plenty of leisure in which to repent it and indeed the next morning

I was sick and my neck was covered in love bites.

And then that very night, we were all off to a gig at 'The Clay Pigeon' pub in Eastcote. I walked up to Zola's house and she noticed my love bites straight away even though I thought I'd done quite a good job of covering them up. Adam arrived and we braved the icy, snowy world and got on a tube to Eastcote. Further to the front of the train I saw Tris and Bee; they didn't see us and walked on ahead because we had to wait a few minutes at the station in order to meet Slimy. At the venue, we went into the bar first of all and just seeing Tris made me feel very up. Then I had to say 'hello' to Bee and felt terrible and Tris walked behind me and clicked his tongue softly as he did so. You can't deny that illicit liaisons have their thrill. We shuffled into the hall to see the band and Tris came in for a while without Bee. He chatted to a large group of us whilst I drank copious amounts of cider and began to feel a lot better. At some point, Peg ambled over to me and apologised for his outburst the previous evening. Then in the toilets I collided with Bee, we sprayed and back-combed our hair companionably together in the large mirror and she was very friendly and unsuspecting. I knew I was a bad person but I still couldn't bring myself to regret what for me had been a fantastic experience. At the end, a group of us walked up to the station having snowball fights along the way and I linked arms with Janet 'Blue Hair' to sing Cream's version of 'Mother's Lament' complete with the *'d'you want to do it again?'* tag line, at the top of my voice (and I really cannot sing). Tris came along on my side of the road, whilst another lot that included Bee were on the other. With his long stride he easily caught up with us and told me that he'd just finished with her. What on earth for? 'I hope it isn't my fault', I said.

He said it wasn't and Jimmy Hill's beard flew by. We spoke again as we came down the steps to the platform, and in the waiting room, with its rusty old heaters going, he sat on his own miles away and looked tortured. Bee seemed okay, but I guess she was putting a brave face on it. The train chugged in and we all got on. 'Cheer up', I said to Tris as we took our seats and he squeezed my waist as an answer.

Then we went and sat as far away as possible from each other. I got off at West Harrow by myself because everyone else was going on to Harrow and as the train pulled out of the station our eyes met like a scene out of 'Brief Encounter.' It was ridiculous, it was melodramatic in the extreme and it was childish, but at the same time it appealed to me because it was deeply moving and exciting. I truly believed at that moment that he genuinely felt something important and perhaps he did, but his love of drama was always stronger than his love for me. When I got in I watched 'Spitting Image' on TV, then had a restless night worrying about everything and wishing Tris were still in my bedroom. The next day, Seamus rang me and said, 'Bee and Tris have split up.'

'Yes, I know.'

'What happened with you two at the party? I saw you together.'

'Oh, nothing much.' Lie, lie, lie.

Bloody hell, why couldn't I keep my hands to myself for once? Now I'd got caught up in another mess and to cap it all, why did I have to like the guy so much? Oh, how I was enjoying my despair. Meanwhile, Foundation, Philbert and Duncan had formed a band and were going up to a ruined church in Stanmore to have some photographs taken. I renamed them the 'Goth Squad' and went up there at Foundation's behest. He kept putting his arms around me even though I'd chucked him, he was trying to be sweet and I just felt ill.

On Valentine's night (no I didn't get any cards), Bee and Tris were in the pub and I thought they were back together, but no, they were trying to do this civilised thing. The result of this was that she looked rather tired and over wrought and spent the whole night talking to him. Everyone else thought they were still together, she ruined her own chances of somebody else chatting her up and no one could get near him without killer glances from her. To add to this, he felt more secure and as though he hadn't really lost her, so consequently neither of them was being called upon to make any adjustments to being single. He was of course playing his games. I looked over at him and realised that he wasn't really that great looks wise, certainly not what I'd call my 'type' any way and I often told him that too. After a bit we all got drunk and he started following me about, getting cocky, mentioning my bedroom and saying how virginal I had looked in my white dressing gown. I wondered if he was enjoying being shitty to her but even so I quite liked the attention I have to admit. Meanwhile, some wanker nicked the umbrella that I'd bought for Peg and that made me very cross. At the end as we straggled outside, Bee was glued to Tris and trying to get him to go back with her and I'd been thinking the same thing so I bet he felt like Harrow's super stud. Pinz came up to me and told me she'd just seen Dennis who'd told her there was a party on at Shuggy's place, so I said I'd go to that. Tris sidled over, 'I'm going home to get an early night' he announced. Have a nice time then. I linked arms with Sharon and went sailing off into the dark shouting, 'I want Dennis' without a backward glance. You want drama? You can have it.

I breezed into the boring hippy party and flirted

outrageously with most of the males. I felt very bitter and twisted because I could've taken at least three of them to bed, but I didn't want to at all. How annoying it is when you want someone but it's always a specific individual and other people just won't do. Dennis was his usual drunken self, yet now of course, very friendly. I felt that he was just too old for me and I couldn't bring myself to do it, even though I had once loved him so much. I wondered if maybe I could still fancy Peg, but knowing that he didn't want me anyway had put me off the idea. A little blonde Casual who was always after me came up and I had a kiss with him and Sharon got chatted up by an old hippy called Frank who was wearing a pink and green spotted bow tie and I kept asking him if it span round and told jokes. It really was boring and I was saying things to Sharon like, 'How to have fun with old people.' The music was very soft, hippyish and non-descript and I believed that the people listening to it were just the same, with no fighting vibes at all. I went up Sharon and sang in her ear, '*I wanna be...*' '*Anarchy*', she sang in reply and with that we escaped into the night.

I got into bed, died in a drunken stupor and awoke the next day feeling terrible. Then the postman thrust yet another envelope marked 'Peckham' through the letterbox and as if by magic I was immediately restored to health. This time it was a six-page epic that I had the privilege to receive from this clever fellow. The first page was an official typed letter from the department of employment, a UB 78, no less, that he had filled in as follows:

Dear Sir [crossed out] Madam
I urgently need to know the number of calendar weeks in which the person named overleaf has worked as an

employed earner for at least 16 hours in each week (21 hours in weeks before 3 April 1978) since the date stated.

Accordingly would you please complete the declaration overleaf and return this letter as soon as possible.

Yours faithfully

**Mr Fascist**
Manager [crossed through] **Cunt**

Page two, consisted of a script designed to look as if it were made from newspaper cut outs like a blackmail letter and read.

> **Dear Nettie,**
> **We have**
> **your underwear,**
> **and we're not**
> **afraid to**
> **use it.**

The following page had a biro drawing of a pair of knickers speared through with a dagger, above which was written:

*If you don't leave a picture of Shakin' Stevens and 300 Lira in a brown paper bag in the 3rd cubicle of the Gents on Waterloo Station, photo copies of said underwear will be sent to The Soviet Embassy, Reader's Digest, The Acton Evening Echo & Commissioner Newman of The Metropolitan Bacon Emporium. You have 3 days to pay or else...*

Page four went like this:

*Big Boy Primary School*
*Hanger Lane*
*E33*
*Dear Miss Baker,*
*It has come to our attention that over the last few weeks several of the youngsters have been coming into classes late in the afternoon with abnormally large quantities of Toffees, Spangles, Hula Hoops and Smarties stuffed down their Y-Fronts. When questioned about this they explained that you had given them the sweeties only if they would walk barefoot on your back singing the chorus from Roscinni's 'Barber of Seville'. Not only is this behaviour unacceptable but I feel the fee charged is far too low. May I suggest a payment of 3 bars of Fruit and Nut, 2 Crème Eggs and a Marathon? If you agree to these terms I shall be happy to meet you, say, Thursday lunchtime by the bike sheds.*

*Yours*
*Sincerely*
*Mr A. Nuss*
*Headmaster.*

Next came page five:

## BEFORE YOU READ THIS YOU HAVE ALREADY WON A PIECE OF CHEESE AND A TOILET ROLL.

*Yes, unbelievable, but true. This totally worthless piece of Bog Roll is your ticket to the chance of a lifetime. Just fill in the back, throw it in the bin and say to yourself 'what a fuckin' waste of time that was.'*

*This piece of paper was distributed on behalf of The Really Annoying Circulars Company* ™

Finally on page six, whilst wiping the tears from my eyes, I got a small amount of sense.

*But Seriously,*
*Hope you're keeping well. Its amazing the crap you write when you're bored at work. By the way, like the new psychedelic Civil Service notepaper? Groovy huh?*
*Not been up to much excitement lately, in fact life has resorted to TV, books & boredom due to lack of financial stimulation. One piece of good news was me bike passed its MOT so I've just got to get me tax & insurance and its...*
     *'Born to be wild'*
*Watch out Peter Fonda, Eddie Kidd and Batman coz Mad and his 100 cc Blue Meanie will hit the road.*
*I've got to pack this job in soon, its really starting to grate. Think I'll kill the manager first. Will see you soon,*
*Luv MAD XX*

And that is apparently how some of those working in the Department of Health and Social Security whiled away their working day. This amusing epistle led me to think of Mad as the most intelligent bloke I'd met even though he'd strung me along for ages with no action. I wondered if I really should have waited for him instead of getting so desperate and insecure that I ended up doing silly things like Tris. Ah, if only I had, but it was too late now. Anyway, I wrote straight back just in case. You must always keep your options open.

On Monday 17th February, I took some more speed and

went off to a Flowers in the Dustbin gig at The Fulham Greyhound. As soon as I walked in I bumped straight into Bee and had an attack of paranoia. Tris was on the other side of the bar, but took a rather circuitous route to the bogs in order to talk to me and tell me that she had no idea about us. I continued to drink away merrily and then had some Amyl Nitrate for the first time since The Bell had rammed some up my hooter at the Widmer Stud party when I was eighteen. I discovered that if you just wafted it under your nose like smelling salts, then you could actually get quite a pleasant buzz off it without feeling as though you were about to pass away from a cardiac arrest. QOS then asked if we'd like to go back to hers afterwards, so I invited Tris and he seemed keen on the idea. I wasn't too amused though to notice that both Horsey Helen and Bee were hanging around him. I imagined that once I started to like someone then everyone else wanted them and how I hate to have competition. Meanwhile, Foundation and some creepy hippy followed me back and I was totally out of it and trying to play it cool with Tris by standing miles away from him. Bee thought that Horsey Helen was after him, though personally I would have said that it was the other way about. Nevertheless, I quietly held my ground and when Adam said that he thought I should stay there because he didn't want me to walk back by myself, Tris volunteered to take me. He sat on the edge of the four-poster bed and said that he hadn't imagined that he'd be back so soon, but he obviously hadn't reckoned on my determination to get what I wanted. The language of love truly did slip so easily from his tongue and when I was with him I believed that he was my protector and that he alone could save me. He loved to say, 'I am not Spock, I am an actor', and then, because he bloody was Spock, 'Live long and prosper.' Inevitably, as the banter progressed, I became 'Jim Kirk'. At five pm the next day he went off into the snow. That evening both Peg and Foundation phoned me. What did they want? They wanted to come round, so I said 'Okay.'

In our new house, an Irish builder named Joe had started work on a loft conversion so that my poor brother could actually have a bedroom of his own and thereafter the mornings became punctuated with crashing and banging for some weeks. I went off to a gig up at The Fulham Greyhound where I met up with the 'in crowd' who gave me a lift home and we stopped for fish n' chips on the way. The following day started as usual with a mild hangover and the builder in the loft. Several males and females phoned me for support and advice. Peg came over and Mad phoned wanting to know why he hadn't been invited to Leda's eighteenth birthday bash, which was scheduled for the 20th Feb. 'How did you find out?' I asked. 'I have my sources,' he replied.

The 'source' was of course Tris and I did wonder what on earth he thought he was playing at. Two horny ones at once was a bit much to deal with... as if, ha ha, that was really going to happen to the likes of me. True to form, I agonised over it all and got very excited singing and dancing about to 'Clash' and 'Buzzcocks' songs all the live long day. On the night in question, Tris turned up on his own and I was actually glad to have been spared being put in a difficult situation as well as to have him behaving in a quite a 'boyfriendy' sort of a way. He spun me the story that Mad had found about the party 'by accident' and that he'd managed to talk him out of it. I went on to get so drunk that I set my mohican on fire whilst lighting a cigarette from a candle and Tris rushed to put it out for me; not that I noticed or even cared by then. He spent the night again and when he left me he said, 'This is becoming habit forming.'

At a gig of Hig's at The Roxborough the next night, Tris

turned up again looking very good. At the end he said he was going home but he followed me up to the junction. A post apocalyptic vision of two bizarre looking Punks trudging along over the ice, as a freezing wind moaned around us through the bleak, dark streets of the half demolished town.

'Give me a kiss,' said a voice from behind me.

'Why'?

'I don't know.'

But the following evening he appeared at the pub and asked, 'Is Bee here?' causing my heart to plummet a million miles.

Sure enough, there she was and they spoke for quite a while. Adam caught my eye and we exchanged smiles that recognised the incongruity of the situation. Later on, for some reason that will remain forever unexplained, Tufty confided in me that he was, 'Not drunk' but was nevertheless, 'Well out of it' and was worried because apparently he had to drive. Then he and Zazie went outside and got into his battered old orange Volvo that was parked across the road. Presently, the sound of squealing rubber served to alert us drinkers to what was now occurring beyond the windows and we all rushed to the door in time to see Tufty reverse very fast indeed the wrong way up the street and smash dramatically into a poor little red Golf that was parked by the kerb. He then continued backwards away from that carnage and roared across the road, with smoke billowing up from his melting tyres, where he smashed into some railings and then almost collided with another car going correctly round the one way system of what is now sadly a wholly pedestrianised area. We had all by this time completely forgotten our own worries as our jaws hung open with amazement. Tris was standing right behind me as we loudly implored Tufty to, 'drive away quickly before a pig van comes along!' Which he did eventually after a bit of time and confusion. Crikey, that was exciting.

We discussed these events on the way home as Tris followed Tim and I along the road. At the music shop he stopped to look in the window and we walked on and crossed the temporary car park space that the recent demolitions had created and I kept asking poor Tim what he thought I should do. We walked back to the shop where Tris stood smiling in triumph and we three then went off down The Pinner Road. We passed Pinz and Philbert kissing outside the gates of Cunningham Park and then I went for a wee in the graveyard, with my own chains jangling enough to wake the dead as I scaled the locked wooden gates. Tim veered off home at the zebra crossing and Tris followed me to the end of my road.

'Right, this is where I put my foot down.' Said Mr Masterful, so I started to walk off. 'Come here!' he commanded, as he sat down on a red brick wall that bordered the front garden of one of the terraced houses. He winked at me. 'Do you want me stay the night or what?' 'Yes.'

Apparently he'd only gone home the previous night because I hadn't asked him. Men.

Back at base he and my brother sat and talked about drums for hours on end, which didn't thrill me that much. When we finally got to our own talking he told me that soon he would tell the world about us, but not yet because he didn't want everyone to think I'd stolen him from Bee. The next afternoon, we walked up to the end of the road together.

'I've got your phone number,' he said.

'I was going to say something about it, but didn't.'

'Not that I'm going to ring you up anyway,' he muttered quietly, adding, 'I got it from Leda's advert in the NME.'

'That's cheating.'

Then he kissed me and walked off. 'See you.'

Aaaarrrgggghhh! Well it was my own fault. I went off into a snowy day to have tea with Zola and forget about it. Later on 'The Box of Chocolates' came round (a new name for Flying Eyebrows and Brian) and Eyebrows asked me if there was any gossip, to which I thought, 'Blimey, if you only knew you'd have a field day!'

And as usual, there was even more excitement on the way for the Bakers. Because a couple of days later, South Harrow Police Station rang us up at about half past one in the morning. This was to inform Mum that they'd picked my brother Kofi up for possession of hash and that as he was under eighteen, they wouldn't let him out until she went down there in person to claim him. It was once again a freezing and icy night and Mum had to turn out and get a cab, doing a Muttley the dog type 'snacken racken' swearing under her breath all the while. The plods had apparently apprehended my poor bro, just at the end of our road and homed in on him because he was carrying his snare drum and they thought that surely he was a burglar. He only had about two joints worth of blow on him, but there you go. So Mum duly arrived at the Police Station and said, 'I've come to collect the dangerous criminal.'

This did not go down too well with the boys in blue. They insisted on grilling Kofi as to where he'd scored the gear and Mum told him not to tell them, which annoyed them further. Then they quizzed her about us other children to find out if we were under age and could be taken away. They wrote, 'Mother unco-operative' on their piece of paper and said that if she didn't become more conciliatory then this would result in Kofi being charged. They did get out of there in one piece though and this incident resulted in Tufty referring to my brother as, 'The Drugs Baron of Harrow,' for quite some considerable time afterwards.

A few weeks later Kofi received a caution for this terrible misdemeanour and the law requested that a person aged over twenty-one and with no criminal convictions, must accompany him to hear this ticking off. So I went along for a laugh, dressed in a black leather skirt, with fishnet stockings and proceeded to cross my legs in front of the cautioning officer (no, not like Sharon Stone).

Meanwhile, in the intervening period Mr Melodrama (Tris) had been getting the maximum effect out of our affair. As I walked into the pub that Friday, he immediately grabbed my arm and said, 'You'd better hear this as well.'

Because he had apparently and without consulting me of course, told his singer Dave about us who had got drunk and told Mad who just happened to be with his legitimate girlfriend at the time, who wasn't too amused. Children honestly, as if anyone cared! I thought it was pathetic. However, I was secretly impressed that this had all happened before Leda's birthday and was the real reason Mad hadn't turned up because Tris had already staked his claim. He came home with me that night and once again I was amazed at how well we got on. The concept that you could actually be friends as well with someone with whom you are attempting to have a relationship was a new one to me. However, I had reckoned without Bee, who had quickly changed in my mind from the person I'd betrayed, into the enemy and Tris didn't help matters by continuing to be very friendly to her. He soon realised that he had sufficient power to keep us both tortured and on the go and he lost no time in exploiting the situation to his full advantage, whilst at the same time claiming to feel (perhaps genuinely as he was only 19) confused about it himself. For the time being he was with me, whilst she shot me looks that could kill and bought him drinks and pretended to him that she didn't mind. You might ask yourself and indeed I should ask myself if I weren't old enough to know better and why on earth would I put up with such crap? Good question, but I guess that any emotional existence beats living in the void. How tedious life can be when you continually seek to shield yourself from pain, what's the point of that and how can you ever know happiness if you haven't trailed through loads of shite? I was having a brief spell of joy and I recognised it as such.

The streets remained blanketed in snow and Tris and I had a massive snowball fight with Tim and Matt on the way back from the pub one night. Then they pushed me down the road in a shopping trolley and we picked up traffic cones and threw them about, which was very naughty and delinquent of us. Dennis and a mate had decided they were off 'to find themselves' in Thailand as the hippies were wont to do and they had a farewell bash down at The Roxborough that I attended. Dennis was looking at me all night and at the end he proceeded to stick his tongue in my mouth and we had a big snog much to the surprise of everyone. I truly wished him well and hoped he might grow up a bit in the process (I could talk), but as it transpired, he was just as big a drunken loser when he came back, as he was before he went away. After buying some food, Duncan and I got a cab back and won a quid bet off Leda who had insisted that she could beat us back to the house on foot. Once at home we smoked loads of joints and a water pipe and listened to Jethro Tull's 'Stormwatch' album, which made me feel very sentimental about The Bell and that just shows you how extremely out of it I was!

The very next day it poured with rain, the snow melted and lumps of slush rushed along the gutters and got washed away down the metal gratings of the drains. Duncan came round again with supplies and we sat down to watch the film 'Excalibur' on video. Unfortunately, if you are familiar with 'Monty Python and the Holy Grail' these serious takes on the Arthurian legend are not to be recommended. You will soon find your mind wandering to questions about the air speed velocity of swallows and having that irresistible feeling that The Lady in the Lake can be nothing more than an 'aquatic tart' from now on. Whilst we were at least attempting to take some of the action seriously, the telephone rang and Duncan went to answer it. 'Tell them I'll ring them back, unless it's Tris,' I shouted, and I'll be blowed, it *was* Tris.

Things appeared to be going well. Nevertheless, a couple of days later Mad phoned me up and he was very drunk. He told me that he was winding Tris up by pretending to be really pissed off about the whole thing, because he thought he needed a lesson. He asked if he could still come over and see me and yes I was sorely tempted. He obviously knew a lot of things that I didn't because he gave me his phone number and told me I could go over to his any time that things got bad and he wouldn't let me hang up for ages. 'If only you'd got your skates on sooner, none of this would've happened' I told him.

I wondered why I was suddenly so much in demand, and imagined that I was currently a bigger hype than Sigue Sigue Sputnik (who if you remember, were a very silly band with tie on mohicans). Then Brian came round and we spent hours discussing how odd Flying Eyebrows was, then he said that he thought Tris was a real bastard. Oh.

But bastard or no, he continued to come round and see me and stay the night and sweet talk me out of my concerns to the extent that I believed that it was Mad who was trying to ruin our burgeoning relationship at the behest of Bee and The Flying Eyebrows. I still did think Mad was horny though, even if Tris said he thought he looked like a 'pipe cleaner.' One day though, Tris informed me that he was going to a 'Malice' gig in Southend and that Bee would be there, they'd be thrown together and he was 'worried about it.' Now why wasn't I invited you have to ask? I have no idea, other than the theory that perhaps they'd booked up tickets and coach a while beforehand and/or I couldn't afford it. I don't know why he had to even mention this concern to me if not to a) worry me and b) excuse himself for something naughty he was already planning to do! Flying Eyebrows and Brian came over again and she mentioned Bee non-stop as well as trying to get me off with Mad again and I wish I'd bloody let her. I understood that my flimsy relationship was under pressure from the mob but I thought we could withstand it in the light of the regard we had for each other. Ha ha.

The day arrived that Tris went off to Southend and I went off the The Royal Beard as usual. Sandra immediately caused my doubts to resurface by saying that if she were in my situation, she would go mad about her boyfriend being away with his ex for the night. But what could I do about it anyway I wondered? It was his life and if he wanted to go back to her he would, but the rest of the night was ruined for me now whatever the outcome.

Now you won't be surprised to learn that of course he did do things with her in Southend and with all the subtlety of youth he came over and told me about it himself the very next evening. I couldn't really complain could I, because I'd started the whole thing and I knew that I deserved everything I got. I just said, 'I knew you would. Go back out with her, I don't care,' in a very matter of fact voice.

'But I don't want to,' he replied.

In fact she thought it was all back on and had got him to agree to chuck me, which he was going to do until he saw my beautiful face again (!). He was muddled and over influenced by women. Nevertheless, we survived that mini trauma, were soon back on our happy track and our next outing was to a gig that Leda was doing at the Thames Poly over in Woolwich. She had recently joined the psychedelic punk band 'Rubella Ballet' as one of their guitarists and Mum, Tris and I went along to lend our support. I was more than happy to leave Bee and Harrow far behind me for an evening and have the man to myself without old Hawkeye giving me the evils. We traipsed in to this very dark venue that was stuffed to gills with multi-coloured mohicans just as Sweet's old hit Blockbuster was booming out of the speakers.

'You better look out, you better beware, you better watch out if you've got long black hair,' sang Sid, the very tall drummer, to Mum and I as we greeted him and his partner Zillah, the lead singer.

Tris was the perfect escort, good natured and attentive — his massive presence delightfully reassuring as he stood behind me. Leda broke a string and Mum took some great photos. But back at home Tris insisted on going over the salient points of 'the saga' again, saying that we mustn't give in to Bee and 'fall into her trap' and that I should write to Mad and tell him 'a few facts'.

Mad and Tris did get to be briefly okay with each other again, but Flying Eyebrows got on my nerves so much by coming round and talking about Bee all the time, that I was keen to say, 'Please piss off' and it was only the fact that I liked Brian so much that prevented me from doing so. I believed that Tris was a good friend to me and never ceased to be amazed that having a boyfriend who was also a mate was a possibility in life. We went to gigs aplenty at The Clay Pigeon and The Pumphouse. Little Tris and

Mikki came and stayed and the mad March wind blew shop signs about all over the place, put carrier bags into orbit, sent branches flying off trees and propelled next door but one's fence and garage doors to the opposite side of the road. I said, 'who cares about futures? I only live for now' and I was very happy.

On Thursday 27th March, Tris's band Night Music did a gig at The White Horse pub in Brixton. There was a strange atmosphere in the run up to this event because he was going to be staying over there but I wasn't. Furthermore, Bee was of course going along to make herself look a prat as usual by turning up and hanging about being pathetic and it was additionally the first time we'd all be together, including Mad and his legitimate woman, since the whole thing had got so incredibly and boringly complicated. On the big day, I hooked up with Peg at Harrow and we got the train to Neasden and met Mum, then she gave us a lift to Brixton where we saw Leda and some others that we knew, as Flowers in the Dustbin were also on the bill. Tris was on stage and there was sad Bee standing right in front of him and I wished whole-heartedly that she would die. However, all was not lost because I had a drunken Peg being very friendly and then who should waltz over to speak to me but the beautiful Mad. On second thoughts, yes all was lost because old Hawkeye had wasted no time in telling all and sundry about how hard done by she was. Consequently, Mad got heavy about it, grabbed hold of Tris when he happened along and all anyone ever said throughout the whole gig was, 'Bee, Bee, Bee.'

Tris got drunk and had tantrums, whilst Mad became a charming, dangerous and wily old fox and Peg went on about his troubles as per usual, hardly noticing that I was actually experiencing some of my own. To cap it all, the band never got paid as someone had 'allegedly' half inched the dosh. What a bollocks night that turned out to be, though I have to say that Mad's girlfriend managed to behave in a polite and civilised manner for the whole evening, probably due to the fact that she was so elegant and attractive that she considered us outsiders from the north to be beneath her contempt. I was still after her bloke though and in fact I wrote to him the very next day. Never put all your eggs in one dodgy basket.

In the real world of health and things you really ought to think about, I was having trouble finding a decent doctor to prescribe me the contraceptive pill. One silly old windbag of a woman had said, 'You can't be on it forever you know?' and I nearly laughed in her face.

I decided to pop down to The Family Planning Clinic in South Harrow and as I hadn't had a smear since I was twenty. They insisted on doing a full MOT whilst I was there and I thought that was the end of it. In romance world, Tris's band Night Music, were planning another away gig at a place called The Riverside, which was a night club in the vicinity of the town of Leatherhead, in darkest Surrey. You would have thought by now that I would have learnt my lesson about their away gigs especially as bloody Bee was going to be there again wouldn't you? Straight away there was some doubt about whether I'd be allowed to go or not. Tris's excuse being that there would be no transport for me and he would feel responsible, but then he told her the very same thing. When she informed him of her intention to be there he said to her, 'but you won't be able to get back.'

'Mad will look after me,' replied the little cow [get off, he's mine as well!]

'I hope you'll be very happy together' [not jealous then]

'Piss off!'

How do I know of this private conversation you ask? Because he told me and deep down I knew my days were numbered. Bee was a girl with a beautiful face and I was merely a 'Wabbit'. After another week or so in which my romance continued to flourish under the troubled skies of Bee and Mad stirring up lots of problems, the day of the gig arrived. Tris and I waited for half an hour in the cold at Harrow Met for Peg to arrive, which he did eventually, bringing several beers with him so we weren't too cross. We three got the train to Elephant & Castle and then a bus to Peckham and I finally got to see the famous address in Danby Street to which I had been corresponding for so long. Quite frankly, I was terrified of the other girls, but luckily they were okay to me. For the journey to the club, most of the gang squashed into the Transit van with all the equipment, whilst Tris, Peg and I went along in a car driven by a bloke called Chris. But the bandwagon failed to start due to a flat battery and they had to commandeer some jump leads in order to get it going and in the middle of all this there was bloody Bee making eyes at Tris. After a long drive we arrived at this club, situated slap bang in the middle of a muddy field in Fetcham. Inside, a few local yokel mohicans hung about the bar; then Mad came over and said that he wasn't happy, though when I gazed at his beautiful girlfriend I failed to understand why he would even want to look at either Bee or I when he could have her? I'm quite sure that there was something else going on with that of which I remain forever unaware.

Luckily, I had taken some amphetamine and this helped me to cope with the horrible evening that I spent getting stuck at the bar with Bee. Firstly she apologised to me for being so awful and then proceeded to inform me that Tris was the only man for her and she wanted to go back out with him and to marry him. She said he had told her that he only wanted to be free and not see anyone and then she found out he was seeing me. I said, 'Well that's men for you.'

Dear old sulphate made me feel generous, benevolent and inspirational. Yes I could give away all that I loved to the rest of the world without giving a hoot about it. Oh Bee if you want him so much, then bloody have him. I eventually left her talking to him, whilst I went to find Mad, who lets face it was hornier by far, but then Tris appeared and placed himself between us, so that put paid to that idea. The harem master had to keep his women in order. Again I thought that the band sounded brilliant, so sulphate must also affect one's ability to hear correctly is all that I can say. I have the video, enough said. Towards the end, the wonder drug began to wear off and my normal state of jealousy and insecurity returned. I was bloody pissed off I can tell you.

Back at Peckham, the singer forced us all to watch Mad's increasingly shaky film of the evening (which ended with a tour of the Gent's toilets), whilst we drank tea. Then Bee went off to bed with Mad, even though she'd been all over Tris for hours. I didn't get the vibe that Mad fancied her at all, and she'd confided in me that she had slept with him the previous Saturday and that nothing had happened. That wasn't the Mad that I knew. To be truthful, at that very moment I could've just about hacked a swapsie, because Mad certainly exuded a bit more maturity than the angst-ridden lot that I had got stuck with. But no sex happened to me that night either, as we were all forced to crash out in our clothes in the downstairs room. Nevertheless, being sandwiched between Tris and Peg all night kept my mind happily occupied. In the morning Dave the singer barged in shouting, 'time to get up you cunts!' And folk began to shuffle off 'til just Tris, Peg and I were left in there laughing as we listened to a succession of girls ringing up their bosses and saying that they were too ill to go into work that day. Then Mad came in, a gangly Adonis bearing cups of tea for us and I said, 'I wish I had a butler that looked like that.'

It was a beautifully sunny day with a bright blue sky and we went out to the bandwagon to take the equipment off to some rehearsal rooms prior to getting the train home. I climbed in the back of the white Ford Transit, with Tris and Peg next to me and Mad sitting opposite, whilst Dave drove us to wherever it was. Mad and I were flirting a bit and what a drive that was with me and those gorgeous three and the singer who wasn't at all bad either. Yes, I wish the clocks could've stopped then and like Dr Who and The Tardis, the white Transit van from Peckham containing those four mythic, painted men and I, would be off cruising the space time continuum forever. But no, the moment passed and we arrived at our destination where I helped to carry some drums up a million flights of stairs and we three headed off after I had rather reluctantly bidden farewell to Mad. We stopped at an Off Licence by London Bridge; then we stood about drinking beer and smoking fags that Peg bought because Tris and I had spent all our money. Three scruffy, knackered, tatty looking punks in slept-in clothes and yesterday's make-up, leaning against the parapet and looking down at the swirling waters of the old Thames, buffeted by the sharp winds of March. As we chucked our cigarette butts into the river, Tris said that Bee was nothing more than a 'star struck kid' and that he'd made his mind up between the two of us. And he had.

# CHAPTER EIGHT
## Harrow Boys

*'Just when I think I'm winning,*
*when I've broken every door,*
*The ghosts of my life blow wilder than before.*
*Just when I thought I could not be stopped,*
*When my chance came to be king,*
*The ghosts of my life blow wilder than the wind.'*
(Japan, 'Ghosts')

At around 8:30pm the very next evening, Tris rang me up and dumped me so that he could go back to Bee. He was so pathetically upset about it that you would have thought it was the other way around. Why feel bad about doing what you want? I immediately rang Mad in a 'drowning man clutching at razor blade' sort of manner and he said he would be round soon to have 'his bath' at last. I went to the pub and told Sandra who burst into tears. Mad rang me back again whilst I was out and had wanted me to go over to Peckham; it's a shame I missed him. It *was* a humiliating time and yes, I know I deserved it but the pain was terrible. Yet in my saner moments I still viewed our brief encounter as an incredibly happy one, we never argued or fell out, it was always perfect and it just stopped. I had a pain in my heart so I took codeines and it went away for a while, but however hard you try to intellectualise your emotions, those primeval feelings just cannot be reasoned away.

The next night Rubella Ballet played a gig out in Barnet and I went along with Mum, Duncan, Zola, Adam, Pinz and Blonde Lisa. I lacquered my mohican up for the very last time; it had got pretty long now and I was still shaving the sides but experimenting with different styles. Consequently, it was an extremely high moke indeed and I listened to The Stone's song 'Paint it, Black' as I did my eye make up accordingly; black, black and more black with an anarchy sign on the side of my head. I wore ripped, seamed tights, odd fluorescent socks, the spiked collar, a padlock and chain *a la* Mr Vicious, a mini skirt and a black cardigan from which all the stitches were unravelling; very appropriate. We all sat with our heads on one side throughout the journey, so that we didn't bend our mohicans in the car. We went to an 'offie' and stocked up, then into this club that was packed with 'haircuts'. The band launched into their number called 'Emotional Blackmail' and dear old Peg, who never expressed much of an opinion about anything, said that it reminded him of Bee. Somebody let off a smoke bomb and due to the fact that the club had a very low ceiling, we couldn't even see our hands in front of our faces let alone the band. Then a skinhead guy came over and kissed me, which was a small mercy that I was very grateful for. At the end of the gig the band got all their money nicked, which seemed to be a regular occurrence in those days. As we walked to the car we saw some bloke get run over; he fell down, then stood up and walked for a bit, then fell down again. Mum was driving a brown Ford Capri that belonged to a work colleague and we dropped Duncan off in Edgware where said wheels broke down and we all had to get out and push it (Cue Adam Ant singing 'Car Trouble' at this juncture). But we only got as far as Kenton when it finally died for good. We pooled our meagre resources and got a taxi the rest of the way home.

Through the next twenty-four hours, loads of very dear mates called me up to see if I was okay and that was an encouraging indication of my worth to them. I faced the music bravely and went down the pub to witness the happy reunion in person because I really needed to give myself a good kick up the arse so to speak. I got well out of it and smashed two glasses and it was a miracle that I didn't get thrown out of the pub. Tris and Bee were all over each other, then he went up to Pinz and told her to tell me that he was, 'Really, really, sorry'. What a berk. 'What have I got left?' I wailed to Peg 'Your self respect' he replied, adding that he didn't think that Bee had come out of it with much.

It was all a great production, orchestrated by the king of drama himself, who no doubt enjoyed his starring role immensely. Gary the photographer got a gold star for getting me home. At one point I lay in the gutter looking up at him and told him how handsome he looked from that angle. Then I got in and phoned Mad again and the poor guy was in the middle of trying to watch a film and then I was sick. I slept in my clothes, make-up and jewellery, took millions of painkillers (well, four actually) and hoped I would die, which of course I didn't. I woke up looking absolutely terrible, but as I said myself, 'Life goes on, unfortunately.'

My ego had taken a bashing, but I knew I would get up again and I did. Pinz got me a cleaning job up at the Avon offices in South Harrow, so that gave me another £17 per week on top of me dole money. I got on really well there actually, learnt the ropes quickly and only got fed up with it when I ended up doing every bugger else's job for them 'cos I was so bloody efficient. Peg also worked with us for a time and he was a sight to behold I can tell you — a tall stooping figure with his black mohican and leather jacket, pushing a vacuum cleaner. He did do something very clever though that made him rise up in my estimation, and that was to get a computer that he happened to be dusting, to pay him £300! I wish I'd thought of that.

Mad called up again to share gossip and tell me he'd had calls from Tris and Bee and we realised that we had in fact been merely pawns in some nasty little game that they had been playing with each other. 'He thinks he's God's gift to women' said Mad.

Then he told me that Tris had said, 'Sorry that I've blown your chances with Nettie.' 'Have you?' Came Mr Fox's reply.

I was now looking for a replacement and at a party after the pub one night; I set about seriously chatting up Tris's brother Steve. Tris was at the party drama-ing about as only he knew how, being with Bee and yet trying once more to ingratiate himself with me, whilst she tried desperately to be my friend. What for? I sat at Steve's feet and we bantered all evening until I said, 'I do hope you don't think I've been trying to chat you up all night?'

'I wouldn't be so presumptuous.'

'Well I have.'

Tris sat on the stairs and watched us leave as Steve and I got a lift home in the same van together. When he got out to let me go into my house I inveigled him into giving me a lengthy kiss farewell. Soon after, I got the most ridiculous letter through the post from Tris that ended with Spock's legendary line to Jim Kirk, '*I have been and always shall be, your friend.*'

Anyway, Mad was on my case once more and informed me that him and Dave the singer wanted to come over for a weekend to cheer me up. I thought this sounded very good indeed and would be a right stab in the eye for Tris when he saw them in our pub with me. When they arrived on the Friday night they were really pissed up and into causing hassle, which resulted in Tris being very bitchy to me. We piled back to my place and Pinz came along as well trying hard to get off with Dave who was a tad nervous of her. Mad was sick and crashed out on my bed, so the evening became reminiscent of time spent with young children who have got thoroughly over-excited, eaten too much jelly and ice cream and you just know it will all end in tears. Eventually, Mad revived enough for some nookie, but I have to admit that emotionally I felt dire about it. The two lads were a right pain in the neck to have about the house because they became demanding and wanted waiting on all the time, which isn't one of my strong points. Then on the Saturday Tris rang for Dave who arranged to meet him but then deliberately didn't turn up. They truly had it in for him but I'm still not a hundred per cent sure why. Possibly Bee had been doing some stirring of her own, who knows? I only laughed a bit when they slagged him off because it made me feel less forsaken. Harrow ran dry of dope that weekend and everyone was desperately trying to score. I was secretly glad actually, because this is the time that 'Mary Jane' and I started to have a bit of a falling out. By that I mean that paranoia began to set in big time whenever I got very stoned, tho' it took me a while to make the connection. In addition to this, I was constantly forgetting what I was on about right in the middle of a conversation and that was most irritating. I still smoked quite often, but over the next year or so it got less and less until I just about knocked it on the head for good.

On the weekend in question, I was convinced that they all hated me and were against me and it was quite distressing. For entertainment, we sat up in my brother's new loft room and played an interactive, role playing board game called 'Battle Cars.' Aye lads, it were fairly simple in those pre computer times, but we thought we were very high tech indeed, throwing dice, acquiring weapons, ammo and motors and blowing each other to kingdom come. Their bass player Simon had also turned up, but the next day all except Mad buggered off, which took the pressure off the kettle and I. I got quite into Mr Mad and his foxy personality. It would be a lucky woman indeed who could ensnare him, but it wasn't going to be me. He mentioned that a drawing I had done of The Grim Reaper was influenced by Alien Sex Fiend and sadly I had to inform him that I'd drawn it in 1976 and got the idea from Aleister Crowley's depiction of Death on a Tarot card, featured in *The Reader's Digest: Folklore Myths and Legends of Britain 1973* which was long before Alien Sex Fiend had even been invented. I realised then that five years could be quite an age gap sometimes. However, he stayed with me all of Sunday and didn't leave until late Monday evening. He'd taken the day off work and said he didn't want to go, so perhaps he enjoyed himself a little bit? I waited with him on the platform at West Harrow until his train came. It was all very casual and then he was gone, back to his own life and his own world (and his own girlfriend).

I phoned Tris to ask him if he wanted his tapes back (as you do) and Steve answered. He spoke to me for ages and really made me laugh and that was a tonic indeed. Tris wasn't in but he rang me back a couple of hours later and immediately we were chatting like old mates and he said Dave had upset him and he was thinking of leaving the band. I asked him if he fancied popping over for a cuppa sometime and he was over the moon. He said he'd get some beers in when he got paid and come round for a *tête-à-tête*! I felt so much happier immediately. He wasn't entirely lost to me and I didn't care what he did with her or anyone else for that matter as long as what we had together could be saved (oh and it was one over on Bee, even if she remained blissfully unaware of it).

Out in the wide world it looked like we really were metaphorically fiddling whilst Rome was burning because chaos and unrest were rife. Good old Chernobyl had just gone off and a radioactive dust cloud was circling the globe. There was also all this trouble about Libya when everyone thought that world war three had started and there was rioting in all the prisons and they were on fire. I decided that I was going to grab what I could, when I could. Would it be Steve or Mad? Ha, ha, as if the choice were mine to make!

Yet summer still arrived, with blue skies, greenery, bird song and blossom and we began to sit outside the pub again on balmy evenings. Tris appeared one night straight from band practice and pulled me off to one side 'for a serious talk.' He wanted to know what Dave had been saying about him because he'd apparently thrown a wobbly and given Tris loads of abuse. I thought that as Dave had just spent the day with Flying Eyebrows that that had probably had more to do with it than anything else. Act Two, Scene Two; Tris leaves the band and exits stage left and I totally fail to wonder if it isn't all my fault. Meanwhile, I could see Bee jealously stropping about out of the corner of my eye as he talked to me. 'Oh, just go and talk to your woman.' I said.

But the next night at a 'Malice' gig in Eastcote she pulled me up on stage to dance with her in a gesture of friendship that I found hard to come to terms with. I felt so bad and was so hammered, that Seamus and Big Lisa had to practically carry me on to the train and once on it everyone behaved very badly throwing bits of lighted newspaper about.

*Inside, outside, leave me alone,*
*Inside, outside, nowhere is home,*
*Inside, outside, where have I been?*
*Out of my brain on the five fifteen.*
*Out of my brain on the train.'*
('5.15', The Who)

We got off at Northwick Park and found a party that was mostly full of wallies. However, a bloke I very slightly had my eye on, Ian Chambers (tag name 'Bean', the other one of the two lads from the stairs at Bee's party) was there again, as well as two very nice girls who saved my life by giving me some speed, thus enabling me to me regain some sense and sobriety at last. Thanks to them I was able to chat away to all and sundry in a most intelligent fashion (!) and set the world to rights as well as impressing (!) them all with my sparkling repartee. We eventually got a cab down to Blonde Lisa's half-timbered, mock Tudor house in Porlock Avenue, where I sat talking to Ian until I got a lift home at seven o'clock in the morning. Kofi played at The Pumphouse later that day, so I staggered over there and encountered several of the hippy lot with their new babies including Dennis's ex, which was somewhat concerning; for them, the children, or the world in general, I'm not sure.

Pinz had yet another birthday (this time her twentieth) and she got stopped by the Pigs as she was coming out of Seamus's place. For some reason the local constabulary really had it in for her, though as I've said before, nowadays they'd be delighted to have a sweet little Punk girl to hassle the life out of rather than a load of knife wielding maniacs, which is what they've got now. Peg also started to piss me off when I had to keep buying him drinks (what happened to his £300?). Then one night he went storming off from my place because I got bored and went to bed. What was wrong with him? Zola gave me a long lecture about pretending to be tough when I wasn't and The Bell phoned and asked me out for a drink. Then Leda had gig in Camberwell, which isn't that far from sunny Peckham, so I rang Mad to invite him.

It was pissing down with rain and the new acid green leaves shivered sadly in its onslaught as I got the 182 bus down to Neasden and met Mum at the double glazing showroom. We drove up to Camberwell and were greeted with utter chaos. Apparently a magazine called City Limits had advertised the gig as being free, so loads of people had turned up and then gone away again when they found out that they had to pay £2.50 to get in. We had brought along Leda's amp, which had just been repaired but we had neglected to bring the cab part so it wasn't a lot of use. Then I found out that Mad had been up there trying to blag his way in and had buggered off, so I rang his place and got him to bring Dave's amp cab along for Leda. Unfortunately, this also involved me having to pay £7.50 at the door because Mad refused to come along without Dave and Simon. Oh sorry, had the word 'mug' not yet faded from my forehead? Mad looked good as usual but was out of it and I proceeded to follow suit. I decided that since Tris I preferred brawn to stick insects (for the time being). I came home and had depressing dreams.

Cheer up love 'cos here comes another party and this time a very good one indeed. This bloke 'Jonah' that we knew, held his twenty-first birthday party in a hall down at Wealdstone. It was fancy dress and we all made a real effort (any excuse to affect yet another disguise). I went as a film starlet and wore my mother's pink, beaded, nineteen-fifties swimsuit, seamed lace tights, high heels, sparkly jewellery and a black straw hat. I got several whistles as I walked up the road to call for Zola who had cleverly done herself up as a leopard, complete with whiskers and a spotted tail. We then went to call for QOS who had decided that she was going to go as a fairy. Bondy was Long John Silver, Adam was a Terrorist, Pete was Alex from 'A Clockwork Orange', Janet 'Blue Hair' was Doris Day (with blue hair) and Pinz as usual, sported the largest purple mohican in the world. We trooped down to the bus station where a million eyes were on us. We got the bus and after having to wait for QOS whose shoe had died en route, we walked into the party rather like we were walking onto a large yacht. It looked very swish to us and although it was a bit overstocked with rellies and grannies, we didn't care because we soon discovered that all the food and drink was *free*! In fact, as soon as we realised this we were off on a spree and felt as though we had been transported to the early nineteen-thirties and were on the deck of a glamorous ocean liner that was trying for the coveted Blue Riband.

Ian had arrived dressed as a pirate with a patch over one eye and then Tris and Bee turned up. She wore her usual tarty ensemble of Basque with fag packet stuffed down her stocking tops and her new grey-ish coloured hair extensions, which I thought looked as though a hearthrug had accidentally got stuck upon her head. But Tris had surpassed himself and came attired as a woman, complete with a long blonde wig that he kept flicking back and he was blowing kisses to everyone. Just after them, Little Tris marched in as a Gladiator, with Mikki a very beautiful, red-lipsticked She-Devil, at his side. The atmosphere fairly fizzed with bonhomie. Adam had a pint under his arm and he and Pete held four glasses of scotch each that they continually clinked together saying, 'Cheers'! Blonde Lisa kept repeating the refrain, 'I'm pissed,' whilst Zola pinched her camera in order to document the occasion and Pinz sat in a corner munching chicken drumsticks until she was left with a large plate of bones in front of her. The music was really 'Fred Dreadful' but we danced anyway.

After a bit, the ugly bird that was in fact Big Tris tried to talk to me, but without much success initially as old Hawkeye Bee kept getting in the way. Eventually we did get together and clicked again and he grabbed my hand and said, 'I've missed you' and I was dancing and Hawkeye was trying to be friendly as I gracefully moved away from her and disgracefully moved in on her bloke. Adam had got into a terrible state, not helped by the fact that his relationship with Zola was perpetually on the skids. He decided at this point that he'd taken a shine to me instead and said, 'This isn't drink talking, I really like you and you put yourself down so much.'

'Adam, you are drunk.'

We sat down on the edge of the stage at one end of the hall and he had his hands all over my legs. 'If I wasn't going out with Zola I'd try really hard to get off with you.'

'Well, you're trying pretty hard now!'

Tris came along and sat on the other side of me and I told him I was going out for a drink with The Bell the next week. 'Oh no, not him!' He exclaimed and grabbed my arm, 'don't do anything with him will you?' 'I might do.' (As if I bloody would!)

I slagged off the boys from Peckham to get him feeling guilty and he sighed, 'I feel such a bastard.'

'Don't be so ridiculous. Bee had her goodbye when you were with me, so how about me having one?'

'Yes okay, I haven't got morals any more, I'll come over in the week, let's make it soon.'

The triumphant hallelujah chorus began playing in my head. I believed I could share him, no problem. Finally, we got organised enough to get taxis and Adam was repeatedly chanting, 'Come in my cab and sit on my lap,' into my ear and I kept running away and thinking it was all highly hilarious. We got in the car with Zola on one side of me and I was half sitting on Adam's lap, whilst he really touched me up and I tried to look very innocent indeed and silently implored God to intervene on my behalf, which he didn't because he knew only too well that I was lapping up every minute. We went back to QOS's where we were treated to the spectacle of a massive row that erupted between Tufty and the young Zazie. She hit him over the head with a cider bottle (plastic I hope), then he hit her and ran off up the road shouting, 'Leave me alone' as she sped after him.

Pikes was there as well, tripping his nuts off, he collapsed on the bathroom floor and Yawn who was still his girlie, couldn't get him up so she went home without him. A bit later he woke up shivering and asked where she was. I asked Zola to walk home with me but she was talking to this extremely ugly bloke from Seamus's band whom we later referred to as, 'Mr Pig.' Seamus sort of said to me, 'Ding, dong they like each other', then he got me a taxi and that was it.

So she bonked him in the front room then went back to bed with Adam who very conveniently said he could remember nothing at all of the previous evening's events and I can't say I was surprised. If he reads this, he knows them now!

Remember my visit to The Family Planning Clinic for the MOT? Well they wrote to me and said, 'Go to your GP urgently 'cos you've got cancer of the cervix dear.'

This was extremely inconvenient to say the least and Zola recommended her own practitioner, a Dr Green in West Harrow. I went along there and this very kind lady gravely informed me that I had what they call *severe diskaryiosis* or CIN III and would have to go to the hospital for a colposcopy.

'How boring' thought I, who with no symptoms was severely not bothered indeed, only pausing to reflect that I always knew that it would wear out one day from over use. At the same time, Tris the Cancerian drama queen, continued to dog my footsteps and I continued to love every minute of his Byronic and self-inflicted suffering. Whenever he got well oiled he would be over to my table at the pub and regale me with loads more rubbish that I fell for, hook, line and sinker. Like this: 'I love you and not a day goes by that I don't think of you. You've knocked me out but you lost out because you are too strong and Bee is so weak and pathetic and I lie to her and only tell the truth to you.' He added that he'd also been trying to keep Steve away from me. Christ alone knows what he was saying to her, I dread to think, but I swallowed every word of it and I'm sure that she did too. Then as it was birthday month again for QOS, that meant a 'Toga Party'. Thank goodness. It was time for the Archer to saddle up once more and with a fresh quiver of arrows at the ready, to go galloping about without a care into pastures new.

*'In touch with ground, I'm on the hunt I'm after you,*
*The scent and the sound, I'm lost and I'm found*
*And I'm hungry like the wolf.'*
('Hungry Like the Wolf', Duran Duran)

I found a very short piece of mauve Lurex that I converted into a mini toga and held it together with safety pins down one side. I wore heavy ethnic jewellery that had been gleaned by mother in famous times and I tied my hair up high in a bright purple silk scarf. Then I took loads of speed and posed for pictures in the garden along with my brother's young bass player mate. I was expecting to have a good night and I did. The mad toga-clad punks of Harrow congregated once again in the little flat, sporting raw sunburn from the day's hot weather. Tris and Bee arrived and he immediately homed in on me and then proceeded to get out of his head. Ian walked in and I thought, 'Oh good.'

Then Steve appeared, even better, so I went to speak to him. Tris didn't like this one bit and came up to make some bitchy remarks, so I just slapped him round the ear! He went off being obnoxious and upset a lot of folks including Steve and they had a big row until Tris stropped off. Steve told me that he thought his brother was a twerp who was totally confused and generally suffering from thickness, immaturity and mental collapse. Ian came over again, so I thought that with a choice of three I was bound to get something.

I felt sorry for Bee as Tris kept leaving her on her own and he got increasingly huffy the more he could see me enjoying Steve and Ian's company as opposed to his. Finally, he lost one of his contact lenses and I said, 'That's what happens when you haven't got your trusty lens finder with you' (a job I'd once excelled at). He ended up grumping about on the landing by himself — not a happy bunny at all after too much booze and amyl nitrate and he was behaving in a very childish fashion indeed. He told Bee that he wanted to go home, then he stormed off and she went running after him. Then Steve overdid it as well. He went off to be sick and ended up lying on QOS's bed, so I was mother and looked after him for a while. I told him not to get so out of it next time, which I thought kept something open should other courses fail. Many other party goers got a bit ill and were dropping like flies, including Mr Pig who threw up out of a window, but the hardy few (me included) kept on going and danced all night. Pikes had disappeared, so the pretty Yawn was now being consoled by Gaz. At last, I decided it was time for Ian action stations and as the first pale light of dawn crept across the summer sky I was to be found once more single-mindedly in pursuit of my quarry, feeling my way slowly inch by careful inch, because this was a quiet one and I didn't want to scare him. We went companionably into the kitchen to make tea, but bloody Zola followed me in there and asked me to make her some coffee. Oh bugger off will you? Ian and I finally ended up in the front room and crashed out, QOS looked in and chucked a blanket over us. Slowly, we edged closer together. The bells rang, as they say and as we intended to finish what we'd started, we walked down to my house at about ten in the morning. My speed was wearing off and I looked like death in the sunshine of a beautiful warm day.

Ian was very shy and he had a phobia about being short. Admittedly, he wasn't very tall but his job as a builder had given his twenty-year-old body a wonderfully stocky and well-toned physique. He was a ginger nut, all freckly and covered with golden down and the hair on his head, which he often dyed either deep red or black, curled thickly at his neck. He was also a grubby, fucked up, heavy drinker, who'd already had his stomach pumped, probably more than once. But he was creative too and he played the guitar and sang. He got embarrassed 'cos he couldn't say his R's and as his middle name was Roland that was a bit unfortunate. Anyway, he left me that day around twelve to walk back to his home in Wealdstone in the blazing heat. He said he'd see me up the Hill later where the gang had agreed to meet to muck about and play charades and British Bulldog. I had a bath and went up there where I sat and got sunburnt and we lost Zola in the long grass and had to call out a search party, but Ian never showed. My body ached and my chin was rubbed raw from Ian's bristles but such battle scars should always be borne with pride. I rang Tris to gloat over my news and he told me that Ian had been known to box the ears of his former girlfriend Dolly. He sounded scarily difficult and that as we know was always bound to arouse my interest. Right away he put me in mind of a cross between Dave Carp and Dennis, so you know just where I'm coming from (if you've read book one) and I wasn't wrong either. If only Steve hadn't got ill is all that I can say, because I was really after a tall dish with a brain, but then aren't we all loves?

*Got a bet there? I'll meet it*
*Getting high? You can't beat it.'*
('Doctor Jimmy', The Who)

I decided then and there with great determination that twenty year-olds were too young for me and that in the case of scary Scorpio Ian, I should try to keep away. But the next night in the pub there he was looking pretty pleased to see me and saying 'hello' with a smile. All my resolutions went out of the window in the wake of Jimmy Hill's beard, which had flown past when I had made them. Ian came and sat on our table with us and Tris kept drifting by giving me the thumbs up sign, which was simultaneously funny and tragic depending on whether you are feeling amused by the ironies of life or just plain suicidal. For my own part I found his sense of humour brilliant until he started to get the hump and put the boot in and said to me, 'you do think rather a lot of yourself don't you?' I thought he needed a bloody good hiding but unfortunately no one was big enough to do it. Ian caught my attention over the noise of the drunken throng, 'Do you mind if I come back to your place for a while?' he asked. 'You know I don't mind.'

Ian and I walked down the road with Tufty and Zazie. He was quite talkative for him and when we got in my brother was there once more with his young mate who must've thought I was the scarlet Jezebel from Babylon from the amount of men he'd witnessed me bringing home. Ian rolled a joint and Leda came in from a gig and sat with us for a while. He left about nine the next morning with the single word, 'Bye.' He wasn't at the pub the following night, but Tris was and he bounded over to me to ask if I knew where Ian could be found. He was more than pleased at my lack lustre reply. He understood then that his harem was still intact and he offered to accompany me to my hospital appointment, which was scheduled for the following day. This was incredibly kind of him and even if he were only doing it to assuage his guilt it nevertheless remains as a selfless gesture on his part. I thought it was a bit sad that I had to rely on someone else's bloke to look after me in times of trouble, but *c'est la vie* once more.

So off we jolly well went to the Maternity wing of Northwick Park hospital, with Tris thinking it a real hoot to be walking in there on my arm and me feeling all bonded and normal for a few nano seconds of time. A very young and handsome doctor gave me a smear test that left me bleeding for three days afterwards and booked me in later for a further biopsy so that they 'could decide what to do.' Then he said that I should come off the pill for a spell (which I did not do). On the way back, Tris ranted away slagging off Bee the whole time and promising me that he would finish it with her. And pigs might fly.

Three days later, I went out to see a band that were playing an open-air gig at Harrow Tec. We all met up at the station as usual, and Adam's newly dyed mohican blazed red like a beacon in the sultry, suburban dusk. Ian and Tris walked up the road together like a good-looking version of Little and Large and I thought, 'How pleasant, I'll have both please.'

But unfortunately when we got to the college we were met with 'Carpet Head the Common' so that put paid to that. At the Polytechnic, the concrete courtyard was not surprisingly filled with arty-farty students milling about, but we had a good laugh despite them. I was so busy in my rapturous lusting over Ian that I have to admit I completely forgot about Tris. After a bit of time had elapsed, Ian began to look over at me and on the way out he skilfully stole a box of wine and QOS nicked a teapot (?) from which the spout immediately fell off, rendering it useless. Ian and I had mysteriously ended up together once more and we got a lift back with Bondy and QOS, whilst Tufty followed on his bicycle. I'd lost Zola who'd run away having a trauma about Mr Pig I think, but as usual I was too busy with other things to notice.

We sat in that little first floor front again, with the squared bay window jutting out into the pretty street below. This is the spot where the escalators now rise up from the cold, dark marble floor of St George's shopping centre and you step off to go and look at boring tat in TK Maxx and at the back of your mind you feel that it was better when you had more to do even if you could hardly afford to buy anything much at all (except beer).

> *'There's a colour picture in my mind*
> *Of the places that I left behind*
> *Broken windows where the wind blows through*
> *Empty shells of houses that have turned to wind...'*
> *'...All the sweetness has been taken out of this place*
> *So many memories knocked down and replaced*
> *And I can't stand to see the shifting time*
> *Taking me further, leaving you behind.*
> *There's a colour picture in my mind.*
> *Oh, we were so young,*
> *we didn't realise just what we'd done...'*
> ('I Remember You', Eurythmics)

We talked whilst Ian fell asleep and finally, QOS once

again threw me some blankets as she went off to bed. Tufty sat speaking into the receiver of the black, dial-up telephone and its kinked cord cast bizarre shadows in the dim light. Ian woke up suddenly; he was soaking wet and cross and complained that he'd spilt a drink all over himself (I'll leave you to decide if this was truly the case or there was some other explanation). He had to take off all his clothes (what a shame) and we put the gas fire on to dry them. We started to get quite friendly and we made our blanket into a tent whilst Tufty was still gassing away on the blower. But after a while, he clearly thought it prudent to vacate the room. Joyous birdsong greeted us as we came out on to the front path together at around five a.m. and Ian had to be at work by seven. Tufty had kindly left the bike for him, so I got on the back and Ian bravely pedalled me home down the middle of the Pinner Road. We passed the locked park gates in the deserted morning and sailed along under a lilac sky as a fragrant breeze ruffled our dyed and frizzled hair. When we got to mine I gave him the rest of my speed and he went off with a kiss and a, 'see you Friday.' I went and looked out of the back door and up into the coloured heavens, where I saw two wood pigeons flying symbolically over the rooftops, wing tip to wing tip. Ah, it's a grand life in my head sometimes I can tell you.

# CHAPTER NINE
## 'Days of Speed'

Before I continue, I'd like to make it clear that Ian never had any deep feelings to speak of for me and that the whole thing was ridiculously one-sided as anyone around at the time would be more than happy to testify. In fact, he said many horrible things about me apparently, although I was careful never to even ask what they might have been and I still have no desire to find out.

Nevertheless, from time to time the illusion wavered about like a mirage that I did occasionally help him in some way. Only we know what really happened between us and seeing as I'm the only one still here, my rose-tinted version will have to suffice. Where were we? Oh yes. Things did not run smoothly and on our next encounter at The Royal Beard Ian went home early, so I got upset and went and hassled Tris again instead. Bee had gone home as well, as she was off on holiday first thing in the morning to spend a week in the Isle of Wight with The Flying Eyebrows (can you imagine?). That left a large and vulnerable, tattooed young drummer hanging about with a bit of time on his hands. Consequently, he was snapped up and whisked off back to my house faster than a lot of electrons whizzing around in a particle accelerator.

As Bee was going to be away all week I stepped in as spare girlfriend for Tris. The next night we all went up to a gig Seamus was doing in Chalk Farm. Tris and I were automatically together and on the way home for some reason that as usual I cannot explain; I climbed up onto the roof of the bus shelter at Edgware Station. We did get the bus and when it stopped at Wealdstone we got off and Tris bought me some chips. Then we continued to muck about and break the glass in some of the phone boxes en route (now you know just who these vandals are). He phoned me up a lot that week and we swapped all the gossip about Pikes being back on smack and damaging his foot through jacking up so that it had gone black and might have to be amputated. I don't have a clue how true all this was but we thoroughly enjoyed it anyway. Tris said he'd seen Ian who had mentioned to him that he liked me and that one of his mates had spotted Tris leaving my place on Saturday morning, so he had made up some cock and bull story of an excuse. I thought it was working out quite well that Tris could have his time to finish with Bee and I could muck about with Ian in the interim. '*The best laid plans*' etc. Tris however, didn't want me to see Ian at all, but I wasn't going to take any notice of the harem master on that score.

Punk world was all and the past seemed far away; but as I was watching *The Mike Yarwood Show* one evening my old school friend Louise English appeared on the screen wearing a blue taffeta ball gown. With her beautiful smile unchanged, she sang Jennifer Rush's 'Power of Love'. Once again I became acutely aware of my own failure to achieve anything at all that I may have been capable of. But whose fault was that? I briefly remembered two girls getting off a bus in Elgin Avenue (see book one), then went for another drink.

The sweltering heat was the only thing now tying those times together, for everything else was different, especially me. Zola and I knew we were in for a bad night that Friday because the picture was lit up. Ian arrived on his motorbike and he got very drunk. Tris started to annoy me by saying pathetic things like, 'Only a bit of freedom left 'til Bee comes back'. Then he said that Ian was being off with him and I noticed that Dolly was being offish with me, though neither of us could work out why. Tris and I had a big row outside the pub in front of Steve and I slagged off Bee so much that he was most surprised. Ian went off on his bike and Tris and I continued to have a big scene all the way down The Pinner Road. At the same time as this was happening, Ian had severely come a cropper up Long Elms when he had fallen off his bike and broken his arm. A fact we discovered the next night when he arrived at the pub with it in a plaster cast. The picture had been lit up that evening also and as I knew I was about to witness Bee and Tris having yet another happy reunion I was ready to be sad. But Ian looked beautifully battered and vulnerable and he came over to me and said so many nice things that as always, all thoughts of Tris immediately vanished from my head. I decided that I just couldn't be bothered to compete with another woman for his favours, so I drank five pints, wrote my phone number on Ian's plaster and said, 'If we left it to you we'd never get anywhere.'

'Would you like to take an invalid home with you?' replied the little sod.

He was restless all night though and in a lot of pain from his arm so he left around and 8:30a.m and arranged to meet me in the pub at lunchtime but once again he didn't turn up.

Around this time, Zola and I were spending loads of time together and we got into this running gag about Jimmy Hill's Beard flying past whenever any of these guys attempted to promise us anything or meet us etc. We produced a spoof magazine called 'Woman's Beard', nothing rude intended there, just a pun on the Jimmy Hill thing, coupled with the ongoing soap opera of our little lives that revolved around the pub. Everyone we knew featured in it and had some very hilarious and unkind pseudonyms indeed, especially the men folk. Sadly (or perhaps not) none of my own efforts survive, as Zola, when I last saw her circa 1994, said they were no longer in her possession. But 'the woman who keeps everything' AKA me, has two copies that Zola produced to give you some idea. The front cover featured a hand drawn depiction of a glamorous, swirly haired eighties girl, complete with full beard and moustache, reminiscent of Victorian images displaying 'The Bearded Lady' of Freak Show renown. As on most magazine covers, trailers for the contents were dotted about and alerted the Beard goer to topics of vital interest.

- 'MEN – Exactly what is inside their heads, if not brains?'
- 'How to be a bastard if you've been hurt',
- 'Latest in Beer Boy Indie charts!'
- 'And the word on everyone's lips 'see ya later' we tell you what it really means! (Absolutely nothing).'
- 'Competition: Win a night with Mr Pig, Second prize: two nights with Mr Pig!' etc.

'Mr Pig' as you may remember, was the name we gave to this guy that Zola fell for. He was a northerner and he played bass guitar in a band that Seamus was in called Children Held Hostage. Mr Pig was about twenty-three and had been married, but his wife had apparently left him and he was unable to get over it. Consequently, in true man fashion that meant that every other poor unsuspecting bugger that came along had to pay the price for this great sin that they themselves had not actually committed. The magazine constantly pushed this fact, much to our great amusement. One back page featured a maze in the centre of which Mr Pig's wife (renamed

Madonna) sat singing 'Like a Virgin'. All round the maze at strategic points were little figures of Zola (wearing false beards) running about to block his access. At the entrance stood Mr Pig himself, complete with sixteen hole Doc Martens, beer gut, vest covered with dripping stains and an 'erotic hair cut'. Huge red letters proclaimed underneath 'Gosh, isn't it hard?'

Poor Ian, with his height deficiency quickly became 'Napoleon' in reference to Terry Gilliam's film *Time Bandits*, which featured Ian Holm as an emperor who was very keen on '*tiny little guys.*' Due to some shouted abuse by a very drunken Pinz, Tris became 'Balloon Face' and I of course, was 'The Wabbit.'

What you really needed to know was 'How to Have a Good Time at The Royal Beard' and here was our advice:

1. Have at least 4 pints of Holsten
2. Kick people
3. Be sarcastic
4. Flirt with everyone
5. Smoke 500 cigarettes
6. You must go home with the biggest bastard you can find or you will have your Beard Badge confiscated!

Some further 'Do's and Don'ts at The Beard' ran as follows:

Do – have two [blokes] lined up for the night just in case.
Do – Remember to wear your beard at all costs.
Do – pretend to be a girly.
Don't – choose who you are taking home until the last bell.
Don't – extend your three-mile radius without good cause.

The Beer Boy Indie charts had titles that reflected our

current failures and frustrations. Such as:

*'My Carpets not Here, Lets have a Bonk'*, by The Balloon
*'I'm so Confused'*, by Tim and The Skateboarders
*'Have I Ever Told you How Much I Love my Wife?'* by Mr Pig
*'Then Again it's Still Only Fun isn't It?'* by Napoleon
*'When The Boat Comes In'* by James Bolam (the excuse for this one being in was that Mr Pig had bought up all the copies because it reminded him of his wonderful Northern home. Ouch!)

A 'Nookie Page' had extremely unflattering caricatures of the guys and below them scores out of ten for 'in bed', 'looks', 'size willy' and finally their own personal 'bastard rating'. Another page shows a graph measuring the sexual performance of Mr Pig, Napoleon and Midget (a friend of Ian's that Zola liked) and then says that 'I'm afraid Balloon's graph was invisible to the naked eye.' A further rating's page has them scored thus:

'Napoleon and Mr Pig: ... I'm afraid we are unable to give you this score girls, amnesia seems to have hit our reporters.
Balloon: 0/10 (just have to look at Carpet's face)
Peg Leg: 00/10 Well done Peg, a double score of zero!'

Chat up lines fared equally well, who had the best?
'Napoleon' – "Fuck off." Very good, it works every single time, got them on their knees girls. An alternative is a silly grin, which works wonders, 10/10
Mr Pig – "I love my wife", "No", "Fuck off", Brilliant! Works all the time, 10/10
Midget – Doesn't need one, "See ya later" at the end of the night is so brill it works a treat for the next time. 9/10
Gaz – "D'you want to go to the pictures?" Oh dear, what a

terrible blunder (being nice??) Try harder Gaz, dear oh dear. 0/10'

You may wonder why we even bothered with these blokes at all if we hated them so much. Well we didn't hate them at all, we liked them a lot but the prevailing cultural climate was the birth of the 'me' generation. This meant that you had to appear cool and detached at all costs and be seen to be keen to avoid any 'hassle man.' In truth as I've already said, it was just an excuse to behave like a prat, but I have to admit that I aspired to it. One quite sad ditty on the 'Poetry Page' reads,

> Poor old Wabbit and Zola
> They made a long trek to the Polar
> They went there to find
> Some men who were kind
> But they only came back with a Cola

Our attempts at satire helped to diffuse our disappointments and gave us hours of innocent fun at their expense and by the way, they knew nothing at all about it. It's a shame we didn't circulate it more really, but then I guess we really would have ruined our chances for good. Can you imagine what the fragile male ego would have made of our character assassinations? Possibly it was also a shame that such talents (!) should have been wasted as I continued with office cleaning and Zola did the same at another local public house.

Anyway, where was I? Oh yes the Tris and Ian saga. I called up Tris and told him that I wanted it all to stop between us and for the moment I believed myself. I knew from research that Ian was not a womaniser as such. He had had a long relationship with a stunningly beautiful girl called Brigitte who was the sister of QOS's 'friend' Marc. Then he had taken up with Dolly and she had hurt him a lot. I got this from Zazie who also told me that Tris had been trying to find out who I'd gone home with the previous Saturday. Back on the blower with Tris he took his semi-chuck with quiet resignation muttering, 'Ian's been good for ages, let's see how he copes with the pressure.'

'I have no intention of putting pressure on him.'

'You don't have to try.'

The day I'd been given for my next trip to the hospital arrived and this time it was Zola who accompanied me. This was a wonderfully undignified experience, in which a man looked up my naughty bit with something like a pair of binoculars and whistled a happy tune as the light shone down from his miner's hat. He located a cluster of dodgy cells and took two huge lumps out to be examined under a microscope. I was told not to have sex for a month! Are they trying to ruin my career or what? When I got in I rang Tris. He wasn't there but I spoke to his Mum who seemed really nice and I thought it was great shame that I'd never met her and got her on my side because then I believed that Bee would've been right out the window.

The next night I met Ian in the pub. We were very awkward with each other at first but after he'd had dope and I'd had alcohol we got on great guns, or at least I thought so. When I mentioned to him about my trip to the hospital he said, 'I know, Tris told me yesterday,' and that threw me a bit. Then he went off home and said, 'See you tomorrow' (moving up the 'Beer Boy' chart).

So tomorrow saw Zola and I sitting inside as it was threatening to rain heavily. Bee and Tris were there and she'd finally removed her carpet. Ian arrived and he looked so sexy that he took my breath away. I got chatting with Brigitte (his darkly luminescent ex), and we talked about him. She told me that I really was playing with fire and I knew that as usual I was rushing in where Angels feared to tread. He stood near us for a while then went outside. Tris came over for a moment and I looked out of the window at Ian who saw Tris and I together and so he came back in and just stood behind us not talking to any body. Tris noticed this, said, 'Er, goodbye' and whizzed away. I thought Ian wanted to talk to Brigitte. Was this male territory parading? It looked like it to me. Tris continued to catch my eye and kept trying to make me laugh whilst I mouthed obscenities at him. Two blokes (old and not good looking) who had been gazing over at us all evening, suddenly approached Brigitte and I. The ugliest one of the two said to me, 'I've been looking at you all night and you are the most beautiful girl in the pub.'

This was a great ego boost to me but I found it rather hard to believe when I was standing next to someone who truly was the most stunning thing in the vicinity. Perhaps he said it for a bet or a wind up? However, once I managed to escape him I found that his kind words had given me the confidence I needed to approach Ian and invite him back for a game of Monopoly. He seemed quite pleased at the prospect and as we walked out of the pub I noticed Tris giving me a thumbs-up sign through the window.

Ian's mate Midget had tagged along with us as we straggled out into in the rain. Zola was being a pain and hassling him, which caused him some 'stress', because Pinz had behaved in a similar fashion towards him on a previous occasion. All of a sudden Zola just ran off and the boys went, 'Eh?' until I explained to them that this was quite usual and she was always fine the next day. Actually, I liked Midget a lot because he seemed to have a bit more sense than some. He joined us indoors for a cuppa and then headed off into the heavy downpour of a summer night. Ian explained to me that he'd been at Tris's place and had over heard him and his Mum discussing my hospital visit. I in turn offered up the lame excuse that Tris and I were 'just friends', Ian merely smiled at that as

Jimmy Hill's Beard flew by.

The nurse did say, 'No sex for four weeks' didn't she? Oh well.

It was a quieter night, as Ian didn't snore or make noises and only ground his teeth a bit. He got up at ten which was late for him, got dressed and I said, 'are you going up the pub later?'

'If I can get someone to buy me a drink.'

'I'll buy you a drink.'

Mug.

Tris now got Bee involved in the whole sorry tale and she began to make cheeky remarks to Ian like, 'Are you going home, or are you going to get laid?' and I wanted to kill her. Then this same night she went off to a party with Flying Eyebrows without Tris (he probably wasn't trendy enough), so consequently he hassled the life out of me again. I thought I still liked him, which was easy to do after several pints and his skill with the delivery of ten tons of flannel like this, 'I've been depressed since April when I let go the best thing that I ever had', right in front of Ian. Consequently, the atmosphere at the little picnic table began to get distinctly uncomfortable. Midget silently implored me to get a grip, so I went to speak to Ian, but really it was such an effort I don't know why I bothered. However, he said he had my phone number and would call me on Tuesday at eight p.m. and arrange to come round. Oh, not this bloody phone-call story again, I can't stand it. Zola, Pinz and I walked up to the bridge and Tris was hanging about looking for all the world like 'The Anthem for Doomed Youth' as usual, then Pinz let slip her memorably funny 'Balloon Face' line, which unfortunately he overheard so he shouted, 'I know I'm fat and ugly with a funny face!' Well you said it. Christ! They called me 'The Pesky Wabbit' for Heaven's sake and I didn't care. In the meantime I went off to see Pikes, whom further gossip had labelled a hopeless addict on the inevitable downward spiral. In fact, he seemed okay to me, no more or less completely fucked up than the rest of us and we spent a happy afternoon up at The Castle with the hippy contingent. He came back for dinner and I sent him out for a walk up The Hill with Leda and the dogs. I wanted to ring Tris.

Two days later I did just that and Ian (who did not call me on the Tuesday, how surprised are you?) was round there. Oops! That must've spurred him on though because later on he did ring with a grovelling apology and an excuse that his grandfather had been taken ill. He said he'd ring again to fix a date, but then he turned up down the pub sans mates. We chatted all night and the pub population were no longer in any doubt as to which way the wind was blowing with us. Ian asked me if I wanted accompanying home, we had a great night and he left at about four a.m. But then Ian and I fell out yet again due to me giving him 'hassle' and 'stress'. My gloom was once more alleviated by Zola who arrived at the pub wearing a black cut-out paper beard, with the words 'The Beard Lives On' written across it in white pencil. I ignored Ian all night and flirted with Midget, whilst Uncle Tom Cobbly and all flocked around me offering comfort, praise and ego boosting kindness and Ian was universally ignored and got the right hump. I had some power socially and I wielded it this time to great effect. Tris caught my eye then we gazed starry eyed at each other for the millionth time and even though Bee was there, we just ignored her. He was as usual happy to get all his straying sheep back into their fold.

On Wednesday July 23rd 1986, Sarah Ferguson married Prince Andrew and I found it strange to think that I had once known her fairly well. I realised just how far I had wandered from my nineteen-seventies pathway.

For to paraphrase Mr Wilde, I was now in the gutter looking up at her in the stars, which is one way of putting it. I did watch the Royal Wedding and that had the effect of depressing me utterly. It could've been me you know (ha, ha and let's be grateful that it wasn't). Then to cap it all, Ian's ex, Brigitte, told me that she thought he was after Yawn. Great. Then she said, 'How about going for Tris's bro?' Well one, he wasn't bloody interested and two, Tris had threatened us both with death if we even considered it. Midget was nice though.

'You just can't leave it alone, can you?' said Leda.

The hospital was on my case again wanting me to go in for a big cone biopsy thing. Oh, go away.

'I really don't want to get on the wrong side of you' said Ian in the pub that Friday, so that got round me of course and we ended up in bed again. But the next night he ignored me and said he couldn't remember what he had said or done the previous night, which was charming. After the pub, we all went to a party being held by that bloody Pauline gum girl was holding. Then Pauline started snogging with Ian right in front of my face. In those times you were expected to find this kind of behaviour perfectly acceptable, but I have to admit that I didn't. Another very decent guy who really thought a lot of me, kept asking to take me home and I kept saying, 'No, no,' but in the end I felt, 'Oh, so what?' So some geezer gave us a lift back to mine. '*Love the One you're With*'? What utter crap that is Mr Stills, Max didn't know what he was on about and neither did you. It was an unmitigated disaster and made me feel awful, especially with Ian's cold cup of tea from the morning still sitting on the bedside table. I woke up, thought, 'Oh, what have I done?' and went outside to sleep in the garden.

On the Monday, Tris rang and then came round bringing two bottles of cider and a packet of cigarettes for me. We had a wonderful time together and he kept telling me that he would finish with Bee after Reading Festival and pigs and beards and whatever else went flying past as usual.

Later on Seamus did a gig up at the Hammersmith Greyhound, so Zola and I went up there, meeting Tris and Bee at Rayners Lane and they had Steve with them. I found the whole thing highly ridiculous with Tris and I not speaking even though we'd spent the whole day together. I whiled away the entire evening chatting to Steve and Tris threw a wobbly and dragged him away from me at the end. Then Zola had her usual emotional outburst due to Mr Pig's misdemeanours, which resulted in me losing the others, getting on the wrong train and having to pay £6.50 for a cab home from South Ealing.

Less than twenty-four hours later, Zola and I went off to a gig in Chalk Farm at a place called The Enterprise ('Beam me up Scottie'). The lovebirds Tris and Bee were there, so we went and sat miles away from them. He was looking upset and slowly edged nearer and nearer until he could talk about something extremely trivial and banal. When Bee went upstairs to the bar to get him a drink he rushed over.

'This is stretching the point too far.' I said
'Well I won't do it any more then.'
'I wish that were true but I know it isn't.'
'Where's your bottle? You know I don't play by the rules.'

Er, whose rules exactly? Bee was indeed a sad case and still offered me a cigarette even though I was ignoring her, that's what she was like. We got back to Edgware by train and then caught the bus, which only went as far as Wealdstone Garage. Bee got off before us and Tris said that he'd ring her, which caused a huge spear of jealousy to thud into my heart. I jumped from the bus and went storming off on my own. I felt free to be simply walking away from it all. Then I heard the unmistakeable sound of Doc Martens coming up fast behind me. Tris was very out of breath when he grabbed my shoulder and said, 'what the hell are you doing?'

'I'm fine.'

'Well, your best friend is all alone and you should walk home with her.' (In fact she was crying because I'd left her. Oh my Gawd!)

'You are not my master.' (Brave eh?)

'I know, but just do it.'

'Well I'm not doing it!' I shouted defiantly, and walked off.

'Fuck you then!' Retorted my beloved.

A bit later Zola passed me on the other side of the road and said she was upset because she thought I'd been shouting at her. So I sorted it out and we got some chips and were as happy as sand boys all the way home, though it was a bloody long way in high heels.

The job at Avon had unfortunately ended because the firm moved to different premises but I managed to help myself to quite a lot of stuff that got left behind in the clear out, including a decent umbrella and loads of make-up.

On the Saturday I took my hangover up to the double-glazing showroom to earn some more money up there. I needed cash because we had Reading Festival looming on our social horizon and that was to be my last stand as it were before my Op, which was now scheduled for September. I went to the pub and said to Zola that even if Ian bought me ten vodkas I wouldn't make it up with him. I also predicted that Tris would end up as a moody, drunken, eighteen stone yob of a husband one day, because some people can never break away from a mundane destiny. How profound. But then Ian kept walking backwards and forwards in front of me (his arm was now out of its cast because he'd got fed up waiting at the hospital to have it changed, so he'd just gone home and had been back at work all week). Suddenly he stopped and said, 'would you like a drink?'

'Pardon?'

I had a half as I was already on my third pint.

'I've got some really good blow,' he continued, 'shall we go and smoke it at your place? If you want to, just say, 'Fuck off Ian' 'cos I've been expecting it.'

Off we went once more to the accompaniment of Tris shouting derisively at our retreating backs.

As it was the wicked hot month of August, a group of us did a summery thing and went for a barbeque up in Bayhurst Woods in Ruislip. This was the very place where I had ridden my horse Chamango many winters previously and in those innocent days I had cantered along the muddy tracks and pretended that I was in fact competing on Penwood Forge Mill at The Horse of The Year Show. Now I was there with Sandra and her new beau, a guy called Trevor who looked just like Joe 90. An ill-assorted bunch of punks, louts, semi-casuals and the like sat in the shade of a designated picnic spot as the breeze played amongst the dusty leaves. Most of the girls were dressed like Bananarama in high-waisted jeans and off the shoulder sweatshirts, whilst the guys looked like Bros with their bleached, flattop haircuts and vests with the sleeves hacked off. I drank five cans of Pils as the blokes ran about non-stop playing football like a load of twerps. We were making plans for Reading. Lifts, tents etc and this *was* something to look forward to.

The following Thursday, I went out to a gig at a gay club up in Kings Cross called 'Traffic', where they had this one semi-straight night a week. It felt very strange indeed to be a girl in that establishment because there were lots of moustachioed Village People boys about. Bottles of Amyl

Nitrate and tubes of KY Jelly were for sale at the bar, over which were hung notices stating unequivocally that, 'Heterosexual Activity will not be Tolerated'!

We had drinks upstairs and then descended to the cellar to see QOS's band. As I walked through to go for a wee in the sad Ladies toilets (surprising that they even had any really), I got a whiff of familiar pongy Azzaro aftershave. As the whole club smelt mainly of sick, I easily homed in on the pleasant fragrance and there sure enough, at the end of the aroma trail, was Tris. We were so pleased to see each other that it was quite pathetic. He'd come along with the Malice singer Pat and they'd been down there since eight waiting for me to turn up. I was wearing one of Dad's old stage shirts that I'd customised. I liked the contrast of punky hair and make-up with this mad flower power paisley top that was trailing multi-coloured ribbons from its sleeves. I also wore a 'hippy' coral necklace that Eric (Clapton) had given me when I was a child and as if some fey spirits from the other world knew that I was there, the speakers suddenly let rip with Cream's version of 'Crossroads'.

A blond gay bloke behind the bar was being very camp and hilarious. I suppose it made his night with so many straight guys to eye up. Tris came back to mine afterwards and stayed 'til 3:30 am. Here we go again. He was so nice that I believed he really was quite taken with me. He said he couldn't believe I'd gone back with Ian the previous weekend after all I'd said about him. I wasted my breath trying to make him see my point of view and all he said was, 'But you don't have to deal with you.'

As August continued apace and the date of my operation loomed, I was determined to make the most of the coming weeks.

On a Saturday night I topped up with whizz and scooted down to the Beard. Ian was there and he treated me to a lovely smile. Then we all decamped to a party that was being held in a flat over a shop in Wealdstone. I went out onto the balcony part over the High Street, where Tris was sitting swigging from a can of beer. We kissed a bit, even though Bee was around somewhere, but then he started on his, 'I'm not making any promises' record, so I thought, 'Sod you' and I went off to try something else. Ian followed me into the kitchen (where as we know, you always find people at parties) and gave me a long kiss. After that he said, 'I don't know why you bother with me'.

He went on to moan that he couldn't get himself together and that he hated himself for hitting Dolly etc. (To be quite honest with you I felt like hitting Dolly myself on several subsequent occasions, but never mind.) I told him not to worry about it, as what's done is done and we went into the other room where he fell asleep with his hand up my skirt, thus ruining my spotless reputation. After a while I rang us a cab and dragged Ian downstairs with me to find it. On the way out of the back gate we nearly trod on Zola and Gaz who were canoodling quietly in the undergrowth of the scrubby garden. Once down in the High Street, we were alerted by some shouting and looked up to see Midget and another bloke leaning over the parapet. Ian lobbed a can up and they having a lot more ammunition, rained loads of them back down upon us. Just then a pig car arrived, but luckily so did our cab. A policewoman ran across the road shouting, 'Oi!' and I pushed Ian into the taxi pronto and said, 'Drive!' like they do in the movies. Ian decided that we were going back to his house and I felt very honoured by this invitation. He lived in an old prefab down in Ufford Road, Hatch End. His bedroom was predictably the most amazing tip you have ever seen in your life, but I didn't mind, because mine wasn't a great deal better. He had a tiny bed that was positioned perilously about three feet above the floor but we just about managed to fit into it okay.

Ian got up at about 10:30 a.m. and was very lively. He played 'Anarchy In The UK' at full blast, which didn't do much for my poor head. Then he made tea and put The Rolling Stones on. I thought perhaps I should be going home, but he went a bit funny and said, 'You can stay if you like, I'm not bothered.' This made me smile inwardly, so I stayed. We smoked two massive joints and got very wrecked. Some mates appeared on the doorstep so we went with them up to The Hare public house in Stanmore (where I remembered The Loony seizing the gear box on Pete's Zodiac in '78). At one point, Ian and I made eye contact through the smoky, noisy throng and it was heady and powerful with the mutual warmth of shared experience. The pub-crawl continued down at The Goodwill To All on Harrow View and as we walked into the bar Annie Lennox sang 'Thorn in my Side' from the jukebox and Ian said, 'This song will always make you think of me.'

> *'I should've known better*
> *But I got what I deserved.'*

They dropped me home and went off for their dinners and then they all came back for me bringing booze and blow. I ended up having to take the rest of my speed just to save myself from total collapse. Ian kept asking me to give him one of my many rings, so I offered him the one with the silver skull that I'd got for Christmas and I asked him what he would give me in return? 'Myself' was his answer. But then he swapped it for a similar skull ring of his. But then we had a misunderstanding about where we were going next, I got out of the car at my place, Ian looked offended and I lost my bottle in front of the others, so suddenly and painfully we were parted. This was very reminiscent of my losing Dennis that time up at The

Castle and equally as traumatic.

When I got in I had a message from Tris asking me to call him back in the morning. I rang him on Monday and arranged to go over to his place as his parents were away. I walked up Headstone Lane in the hot sun of an August afternoon, passing Midget as I did so and I bet he knew exactly where it was that I was headed. Again, this was my first visit to his house and once more I was not insensible of the honour afforded me. He lived in a large thirties semi in the tree lined *cul de sac* of Parkfield Gardens. When I saw his bedroom a comparison with Ian's could not be avoided. Talk about chalk and cheese. It was very tidy and everything was labelled and perfect. We spent an idyllic afternoon of peace, quiet and harmony, then the beautiful Steve arrived home with a Robert Redford video, 'The Natural', so Tris cooked dinner for me and we sat and watched that. The dream was only briefly interrupted when Bee phoned up in the middle of it, but all that did was to make us laugh, because we knew something that she did not. The fact that Steve was there really made the occasion, for he and Tris were a great double act. We played Trivial Pursuit and Yahtze. It got very late and we drank vodka and Steve and I moaned about Bee. Eventually I stood up and announced, 'I suppose I'd better get a cab home.'

'Aren't you staying the night?' asked Tris.

I walked home late the next day, after Tris had asked me to visit him again and when I got in I rang Ian.

Because I had no record player or anything similar, that night I got my brother to rig up some speakers in my room so that I could put a tape in upstairs in his machine and hear the results in my bit. The wires came down the roof from his Velux window and trailed in at my peeling sash. What I didn't know was that you could also use a mic and be heard through the speakers like a PA. Now Kofi was very matey with Tris and I'd already come home one day to find a sign on my door that said 'Nettie's Knocking Shop' in large letters. So without Kofi realising it, I brought Ian home instead of Tris. As Ian and I got into bed, the speakers suddenly burst into life and a disembodied voice boomed, 'Nettie Baker, what are you doing?' I laughed, but Ian nearly died of fright, 'what's going on man?' he squeaked.

On the Wednesday I went back over to Tris's but the spell was broken. This was because I knew he'd screwed Bee the night before, which caused a quite unreasonable attack of jealousy on my part. Aside from that we got on splendidly as always. We laughed a lot when a TV programme about Napoleon came on. But though I may have taken the piss, there was no getting away from the fact that this particular 'tiny little guy' was the one that I really wanted. The next day Tris asked me to stay longer, but I pushed off without even bothering to mention that he'd said he would finish with Bee the following weekend, what was the point? As I walked along the road I encountered Midget yet again and God knows what he bloody thought, if anything.

Now preparations for the trip to Reading festival began in earnest. I went to the local dope dealer's house down on Harrow View and stocked up with blow. A friend dropped a tent round and then Zola and I went up the Beard where it's true to say that a pre-holiday spirit prevailed. The mad and dangerous Scots Eddie came over and gave me some free whizz, because he knew I liked it. The weather had turned very wet and dismal in time for the Bank Holiday as we all prepared for our journey, but that didn't put me off. As long as I was in sighing distance of Ian for two days solid, that was all I cared about.

# CHAPTER TEN
## That's Entertainment
### *Reading Festival: August 1986*

This weekend consisted purely of sex, drugs and rock n' roll, so Amen to that. On the Friday afternoon, a group of us set off in a convoy of old bangers from Harrow. Adam and Zola led the way, followed by Slimy and his Cabbage Patch Doll, then came Tufty, Zazie, Solo (the dog) and I, with QOS, Bondy, Janet and Pete bringing up the rear. We arrived at the festival site just as it was getting dark and we had quite a to do about getting us all in, which for some reason that I cannot recall, involved me having to do a lot of walking. Eventually we managed to get our respective tents up and then trudged off to the stage in the pouring rain to see Killing Joke. I had hoped to bump into Duncan who was supposedly working there as their roadie, but I didn't spot him and I thought the band were a bit boring. Nevertheless, we were happy despite the wet conditions and Zola got chatted up by an inebriated Scottish man, which seemed to cheer her up. Back at the camp site, the others settled down early, so I decided to go off for a walk with Solo and the umbrella. My rural sensibilities had not deserted me, for I wore my long rubber riding boots and was very glad of them indeed as I waded and splashed through acres of deep mud, my eyes desperately searching the darkened rows of wet tents for any sign of Ian.

Saturday dawned and Zola and I met up with Tris and

Bee. He was moaning on about some awful people they'd come down with and once we'd seen them we had to agree with him that they were indeed complete gobby arseholes. But I was keen to find out the precise area where they were camped, because I knew that that's where Ian would be as well. Tris wasn't too specific but he sort of waved me in the general direction and Zola and I set off. We didn't have much success though and had given up and were walking back, when suddenly I became aware of a 'tiny little guy' bombing across an open stretch of grass towards me. We immediately hooked up with him and his mates Midge and Jonah and with them we smoked some more joints and drank vodka. After that Ian accompanied Zola and I back to our own campsite. The rest of the day enfolded like a drunken, euphoric, hazy and stoned 'Alice in Wonderland' reverie, straight out of the sixties Woodstock era. Ian was devoted and caring and we all sat about loved up and smiling.

For a while the sun came out and it got warm. We got a fire going and sat around it taking speed and drinking and singing and generally looning around. We laughed a lot at Tris and Bee who came by on several occasions. He was looking miserable, which we thought wasn't surprising with blobby Bee trailing about behind him and that's when Ian started referring to them as, 'Mr and Mrs Sensible'. In the evening, we got another fire going and took magic mushrooms and danced about. Then I lay in the tent with Ian whilst Tufty and Zazie jumped around the fire and sang along to 'Bare Necessities' from The Jungle Book. Their shadows cast eerie shapes upon the blue nylon as the fire crackled behind them and the rain began to fall again in earnest. I regained consciousness to the sound of Cream songs floating out into the grey morning from an adjacent tent. You can never escape you know.

Sunday unfortunately, was not as good as Saturday because everyone was on the way down from a massive high. Ian and Midget started the day by taking some Acid, which they said wasn't too good and our happy vibe retreated fast, to be replaced by a strained silence as Ian lost himself tripping and mentally turned away from me. We walked about together and went down to the stage to see Zodiac Mindwarp in action. Finally, Ian uttered the famous, 'See you later' line and went back off alone to his own tent. By this time everyone in the place but me had soaking wet feet and in fact I'd even given Ian my spare socks. It had now stopped raining and had begun to get very cold, as it does tend to do in the English countryside at the tail end of August. I wandered back sadly alone and I was so extremely gone that I couldn't even find the tent for ages and in despair I thought that I was totally lost in all respects. But find it I did by calling the dog, who had stayed behind as guard and he wisely came out and led his useless mother to safety, God bless him. I lay in the tent alone and after a while I heard Pete, Janet, Bondy, QOS and Adam coming back and they were being so silly that they had me in fits of laughter without them knowing it. Zola appeared briefly hours later and said she was going off to find the Ian crew. She reappeared just as daylight was breaking and said they were all crashed out dead in their tent, as you may well expect after the vast amounts of drugs and alcohol we'd all consumed the previous day! On the Monday, we had to look lively and pack our gear up ready for departure. It was very early and we all felt terrible and smelt like tramps. Tufty and Zazie had left the previous evening so I got a lift with Adam and Zola and in next to no time we were home again as if we'd never been away. The only tell tale signs being the usual case of 'festival lip', a sore mouth, dying from knackered-ness and raging hunger. Outside the rain poured down relentlessly on a good old British August Bank Holiday and I was glad it hadn't rained quite so heavily whilst we were there.

On Wednesday August 27th, Malice were playing at The Clay Pigeon and I was all set to dress up and go along. Weather wise, we had apparently caught the tail end of a hurricane, which proceeded to wreak havoc everywhere, rather like Ian I thought. I went up to West Harrow and met Janet, Pete, QOS, Bondy, Slimy, Big Lisa and Mr and Mrs Sensible on the train. When we got off we also bumped into Zola and her mate Linda. I was chuffed to see Big Lisa and we walked along together whilst Mr and Mrs Sensible dropped behind and I threw out some sarcastic comments just to get him sweating a bit. I thought I looked pretty good because I'd nicked Leda's new skin-tight black leggings and had teamed them with very high heels. I certainly looked a lot better than I had done at Reading on the previous Sunday evening when Ian had last seen me and he thought so too when he unexpectedly appeared. Big Lisa and I danced madly and they played 'Brown Sugar' as usual so I could show off my Rock Chick roots. I became drunk and confident and was getting good vibes off Ian so I asked him if he'd like to take a pet home with him for the night? This time his bedroom was actually tidy and I dared to mention the fact that he had got off with Pauline at that party and he uttered that other legendary line of his, 'I'm a bastard.'

The clock radio came on at 7:00a.m. Ian got up and made me some tea. He got ready for work and he rang me a cab and kissed me goodbye at the door and I felt that I could so easily live with him and wash his socks and love him forever.

From here on in I entered my brief sojourn in 'Dreamland' and we began to have a shaky little relationship of sorts, which lasted for most of September.

He'd ring me, see me, be romantic & even put his arms round me in the pub! That night he asked me if I'd like to get up at seven in the morning again. So I beamed through a manic night at The Beard, then Midget gave us a lift back to Ian's where I met his Mum and Dad properly, which I found embarrassing because I felt like a right old flooze. In the morning he was hung over and he toyed with the idea of having the day off, but he didn't and then he asked me what I was doing that night. It didn't seem real. I waited and waited for him at the pub that night and amused myself by being horrid to Tris. Suddenly Stripey and Tim who were outside, began frantically knocking on the window behind me saying, 'He's here, he's here!' Everyone embraced me joyfully, which just shows you how obvious I must make it when I like someone. Tris told me that he'd never believe another word I said, so that made two of us, but he did add that he thought Ian was very keen on me and that I'd played it down. Let's not get too silly and start believing that the world can be a nice place now.

Ian was already at my house having a lively time with Duncan by the time I got there, because he'd gone on his bike and I'd had to walk. The next day he took his bike home and arranged to meet me at the pub at lunchtime. I sat outside the old Royal Beard at a picnic table, on that cloudy, last day of August, with a pint of Holsten in front of me. I looked up from my drink and noticed that Ian had just turned the corner of Queen's House. He wore a Teddy Boy drape jacket over his broad shoulders and he kept on walking straight towards me, all on his own. He got a beer and sat down next to me. But after a while we were rudely interrupted by horrible Dolly. Pah, I can hardly bring myself to write her name. Oh no, she didn't like her Ian seeing me one bit, because she had begun to notice that I was getting somewhere and that was a thing that could not be. She spoke to Ian and she said right in front of me that she wanted to have a drink with him and 'talk to him' and I sat there thinking, 'please go away and don't try to spoil my happiness.'

But hadn't I already done that to Bee? Did I not deserve to get my bad karma right back again? I don't know. Whatever else was going on, she was testing her power over him and I fervently hoped that she didn't have any. Nevertheless, Ian and I left the pub together and began to walk companionably along the road back to my place. As we crossed the car park of Bradstowe House, I mentioned Tris and Ian came out with, 'I'd like to know where I stand, as regards him. It's just that I think he's got a bigger willy than me.' (He sounded serious!)

It was all I could do not to laugh out loud, but I realised that this can be a sensitive subject for men folk, so I managed to restrain myself. I told him some things that bolstered up his ego and got him smiling again. He said that he'd been really happy since he'd been seeing me and I wondered if I was having hearing problems.

We got some cider and sat up in my room talking. Then we leaned out of the sash window and spoke to Mum who was hanging the Day-Glo pink and green socks that I had worn at Reading, out upon the line. Later on, Ian was due to go off to band practice and seeing as he was now in a band with Tris, we found this amusing in a gossipy and couple-ish kind of a way. The rehearsal was supposed to be from seven to eleven and I suspected that Tris had chosen these hours in order to be reasonably certain that he got Ian there in a sober state, but we'd already thwarted that plan. Ian went to ring Tris and he asked him if he could pick him up from my place. Whilst we were quietly whiling away the time he reminded me that I had on a previous occasion told him that he could try other girls but would find none better than me. Sheer bravado on my part of course, but he said that I was right. He also said that if I got jealous about Pauline and Dolly then he got jealous about The Bell and Tris. He told me that Dolly had promised to leave her current flame for him sometime ago and hadn't come through. He said that he wouldn't go back to her now because I had become his 'clinging point', what ever that meant exactly, but I thought we had struck an accord. Yet the ghostly sound of Tris's empty promises echoed in my heart as a warning.

Tris turned up to collect Ian and a comic scene ensued as we came downstairs together and Tris stood by the door. Then Ian spoke to him and Tris looked me in the eye and laughed because we still had a little thing of our own going and this was just the type of game that he enjoyed to play. So off they went together and Ian said, 'See you Tuesday' and I missed him madly the very moment that he was gone.

> *'Dip a dip a dation, my operation,*
> *how many people at the station?'*
> (Playground rhyme)

I'd had to go to the doctors a few days previously to sign a hospital consent form and I'd seen a completely straight and boring consultant. He sat at a desk opposite me wearing thick horn-rimmed spectacles and informed me that if I'd already had children that he would have liked to perform a hysterectomy upon me. 'Oh no you bloody wouldn't.' I thought.

My Mum had often asserted that male gynaecologists were arrogant twits who were determined to have a woman's womb out at the slightest provocation. He went on to say that they would have to remove a large portion of my cervix, so that I'd still be able to have a baby but I might miscarry as a result (to save 'stress' I will tell you that when the time eventually came, all worked normally). So I went into hospital and the next day I sat in bed waiting for the big moment to arrive. I was very keen not to come back with a pack or a catheter as the very thought of these things filled me with dread. From the moment that I arrived on the ward I'd had masses of Punk Rock visitors and so weird did they all look that the staff would just say, 'it's that way,' and point to my ward, to any of my mates who appeared in the hospital.

Practically everyone from The Beard turned up at some point with flowers and gifts (except Ian), which was helpful, but with three recently done hysterectomies opposite me I was a nervous wreck because they all seemed to be ill and dying. Several large glasses of scotch would have gone down well, but now I was nil by mouth and expecting to come back with a drip and goodness knows what shoved up my jacksie. A nurse came round with a form and I said I was an atheist, but then I hoped that God wouldn't get annoyed about that and give me a rough time out of spite. I longed for Ian, but Big Lisa turned up and that was just as good, in fact it was probably a lot better. She was very calm with me as I started crying and told her that I was convinced I was going to die under the anaesthetic. She stayed loyally with me until they came to give me the pre-med and it is kind gestures like these that you never forget.

Now every other bugger else in that ward who was given a pre-med just flaked out completely, but they were obviously not hardened maniacs like myself. I believe that the injection was basically a shot of Pethedine, a morphine derivative, and as Lisa bade farewell to my tear streaked countenance, old nursey turned me over and stuck the spike in. I wasn't really afraid of dying, merely devastated to imagine that I may never experience another mad night up The Beard with all my mates. The wonderful Pethedine very soon dispelled all the worries that I had ever had, as only opiates can do. Far from crashing out, I became as happy and lively as anything and ready to party on down. I joked incessantly with the porters who wheeled me down to theatre, bumping along the corridors with a stream of square white lights passing overhead and I felt as though I were in an episode of 'Emergency Ward Ten'. I'm sure that they found me most irritating indeed.

Once in the operating area, the anaesthetist leaned over me and I explained fairly vociferously that I did not want to come back from the op with either a pack or a catheter in situ. They all laughed and bunged in the knock out drops as quick as possible to shut me up, so that I only got to count back as far as nine (from ten). Next thing I knew I was wondering why they had not yet done the op. I saw a clock and heard a nurse trying to rouse another patient, which for some reason I found hilarious and made some comment about, 'Good old nursey.' I heard a tired voice say, 'Will someone get that one back to the ward?' And off I was trundled.

Yes, all the others had come back from their ordeals, half dead and throwing up, but there was me bright as a button and very pleasantly stoned indeed. No pack or catheter either, so they'd obviously thought the better of it. I felt very hungry but they refused to feed me. I made the nurses laugh and apparently everyone was generally stunned by my liveliness!

Whilst still in this state, I was treated to a visit from Tris, Little Tris and Mikki and just behind them came Ian. Trust them both to arrive at the same bloody time, I could have done without it. Tris thought it very funny to present me with a bag of corn on the cobs, half a dozen eggs and an assortment of bath-plugs from a hardware store. Quite clearly there was a joke intended here, but I didn't find it remotely amusing or indicative of any care for me. Ian on the other hand was a doll, and he handed me a large bunch of red roses, then he stood at the end of the bed and bitched at Tris. He told me that he'd just got paid, so I said, 'You can buy me a present then.'

'Yes, I will buy anything you want.' He replied seriously, though perhaps more for Tris's benefit than mine. He didn't stay long though, I presume because of the dodgy situation, but Tris stayed just long enough to throw in some stroppy remarks about Ian and then say he was going to chuck Bee at the weekend. Yes, we believe you and big fucking deal anyway, yawn and snore. After them came, Sharon, Mum, Adam, Seamus, QOS and Bondy. The lady in the next bed had just had similar to me and she was well and truly spark out.

The next day another great flood of visitors began to arrive in groups one after the other. These included Pinz, Duncan, Zola, Tim, Stripey, Grandma and Mum, amongst others. Finally and most thrillingly for me, Ian and Jonesie (Jonah) turned up well out of it. This time my beloved had bought me half a bottle of Scotch. This went well in tea and cheered me up no end. I was due out the following day and they'd all arranged to come round to mine for a welcome home sesh, so I fervently hoped that I could heal up what the butchers had so wilfully mangled and get out of there. On the day of promised freedom, I had to wait about for the doctor to arrive as you do in these situations. Medical staff never seem to appreciate the fact that being hospitalised is not dissimilar to being jailed (not that I have ever been incarcerated as yet), because you have that feeling of being locked in whilst everyone else is out there having a life. Anyway, I'd unwisely drunk whisky in my tea that morning, which sent the old blood pressure up a bit, but they finally let me out. Yes Ian did turn up that night and my brother let me have the party up in his loft room because he was out. Ian had been singing the Owen Paul hit 'You're My Favourite Waste Of Time' and said it made him think of me. Later on, we crashed out and I woke at six with a terrible hangover. I got him a cab at seven thirty, and then at nine I went down to sign on. I was well skint and even had to borrow a tenner off Grandpa. How to get money? There must be a way and I couldn't even sell my body because it was out of action until October. The concept of getting a 'job' was obviously not an option.

Instead I sat around alone in the sunny graveyard, watching drowsy wasps buzzing about the ivy-strewn headstones and thinking of Ian and I knew deep down that someday he was going to chuck me. The next weekend, there was a gig on at this run down wine bar in Acton called 'Bumbles.' Ian and I went up there on the bus together and he gave me some speed, then he ranted and raved about Tris whom he had recently fallen out with. At the venue, we sat upstairs together drinking at a rough old wooden table until the others arrived. But then there was a fight outside and we all got chucked out and spent the remainder of the evening on the night bus. In between Ian telling me that he really didn't want 'to get involved' (not that old chestnut), he suddenly blurted out, 'But I've given up my band for you!' (Obviously a huge sacrifice.)

We talked around the subject of 'us' and he stressed the need 'to get something sorted out.' Whatever that may be? Of course I did naughty things again too, long before I was supposed to under doctors orders, but I survived and it was necessary to the plot.

# CHAPTER ELEVEN
## 'Another Nail for my Heart'...

...'All things must pass' as me old mate (!) George Harrison so famously said and he wasn't wrong about that. It is now gloriously apparent with the luxury of hindsight that things in our 'punk' world got dodgy because of the amount of substances that we were all abusing and it certainly didn't help much to keep anyone in a sensible frame of mind. Yet as with all great social 'scenes' in history, the protagonists are never fully aware of what they have experienced until it's gone. Ours was the story of the end of our suburban town as we knew it. The transient nature of the squats, of the car parks waiting to be turned into shopping malls and of the pubs waiting to be rebuilt as offices that no one would ever use. All this was reflected in the way that we carried on with our chaotic lives. We were unwelcome in the developer's landscape and certainly did not conform to their vision of a culturally sanitised future that would make them as much money as humanly possible.

Meanwhile Tris and Ian experienced some more serious male bonding issues and as a result of a recent stand off, Ian swaggered about feeling manly because great big tall Tris hadn't punched his lights out. He went and bought some Acid to celebrate and I didn't think this was a great idea. Consequently, I had to spend the whole night with a tripping maniac, whilst I was fairly straight by comparison. I failed to get any sleep at all and in the morning Ian got up taking my last two quid for cigarettes and wasn't even going to kiss me goodbye until I asked him.

'I'll probably see you later,' he mumbled, but about three hundred beards flew past at that moment so I knew he wouldn't. But I stayed in that night anyway due to no money and terminal death. Actually, I *had* started to earn some folding stuff on the odd occasion. This was at a job (who said that word?) that QOS had got me into, and it involved taking all your clothes off in a draughty room and standing very still indeed in an awkward pose, whilst a load of old grannies drew and painted you. Yes, an artist's model! But not half as glamorous as doing it in nineteenth-century Paris I can tell you. Then again, I suppose we weren't too far removed from a world where you slept with everyone and got smashed on Absinthe. But sadly I was no one's muse and it was incredibly hard work keeping still, because you tended to get cramp and thin beads of sweat would trickle maddeningly down your torso.

Another moneymaking scheme that QOS put to me, was that of joining her on one of her visits to a person named 'The Wanker'. As his title may suggest, this was some old bloke who she said was madly in love with her and paid her good money to just stand about scantily clad whilst he had a nice time with himself. After she had informed me that to earn fifty quid I would have to take the whole thing seriously and not laugh, I declined on the grounds that it was beyond me.

One day, I got a call from Ian along the lines of, 'Not that I like you of course, but I've run out of things to do so I decided to ring you.' We hadn't really got anywhere in our heart to hearts except that we didn't want to end it completely. He said he'd buy me a drink but wouldn't stay because he was getting some speed. Drugs and mates came before me, as well I knew and I began to feel that I was too old and frail to keep up with him. Ian never turned up and I began to think of him with Dolly or Pauline and her equally dangerous sister Jackie. I knew that he still had feelings for Dolly and that she had become increasingly concerned about his interest in me, even though she had another perfectly acceptable boyfriend of her own. My greatest fear was that of losing him to her. The next night Ian did turn up and was sweet, but he said he didn't want to stay until I put some pressure on him and managed to get what I wanted. There was a party on at a house in one of the back roads of Wealdstone, so I arranged for Ian to drop his bike off at mine and Sandra gave us a lift down there. Unfortunately, Dolly was at this party and she was very drunk. A moment that I had long been dreading arrived, in which she sidled over to me and started to talk about Ian, whilst an awful blankness emanated from her dull black eyes. I said that I didn't want to discuss it. After that snub, the bloody cow coolly set to work on him right in front of me. Off they went together as cosy as anything all night long and I really thought that I was going to die. Why didn't I just leave? Then I shouted at Ian and he went storming off up the darkened street, so I ran after him. He said that he wanted to talk to Dolly and not to me when I was giving him 'hassle.' Unfortunately for him 'hassle' in huge capital letters was now heading in his direction. He turned to me and shouted, 'Have I ever asked you out? I'm not going out with you!' For that he got a right - hander. Twice.

'You're just using me!'

'You're just using me as someone to treat you badly!' Astute.

'Just tell me to fuck off then!'

'Fuck off!' He hollered and you can't say fairer than that.

I crashed back into the party and Dolly came up to me. 'Fuck off Dolly!'

Dolly started to cry and I fervently hoped that she would die a horrible death (I wonder if she has yet?). Gaz came up and was very kind. He said that he'd known Ian a long time and he believed that he was really crazy about me. I said he had a funny way of showing it. The next morning Ian rang me in a very stroppy mood and said he'd be round in an hour to collect his crash helmet. A very long hour then passed, because he didn't actually appear 'til after five o'clock the next day, when he stood upon the doorstep smiling and asked for his belongings. I handed him his silver skull ring, 'here have this back.' He took mine off and handed it over. I shut the door.

Our separation didn't last that long, but a couple of weeks went by before he got drunk enough to approach me in the pub one night. He weaved uncertainly through the throng and stood there swaying slightly. He told me that although he didn't want to be my actual boyfriend he did like me a lot and we ended up going back to QOS's place to celebrate our reunion. Along with Slimy we took some Acid and the three of us went off for a walk over Harrow Hill in the darkness. We sat on a little bench about halfway up, amongst a line of tall and graceful trees. The curve of the earth appeared to me to be unusually pronounced and the lights in the tiny cottages sparkled reassuringly and nestled snugly close to the earth like the dwellings of Hobbiton. Ian announced that in his opinion I was the best person he had ever met and asked if I would be his friend forever. He rang me the following afternoon, but this time it was a cry for help, as he and Jonah were out tripping in Cunningham Park and needed rescuing. I found him sitting forlornly next to a little fir tree by the gate and he looked relieved to see me. After a brief sojourn at my place we went to the pub and Ian went home, leaving me at the mercy of some determined admirers.

And then the fabled 'Romford Coach Trip' took place. Seamus's band were playing at a club there and they laid transport on for us reprobates. There were about twenty of us on the coach including Bee and Tris to whom nobody spoke. Ian was friendly to me right from the start and he had a couple of the squat boys with him whom we knew as Nig and Pongo. This was my first serious encounter with the legendary Nig and he was the undisputed leader of the gang, so to speak. Nig was very tall, freckly and ginger for a start and as he modelled himself more than a bit on Shane MacGowan of The Pogues, his teeth weren't the best either. But 'Punk Rock man,' that was what it was all about and that night I found him to be a good laugh, if a little out of hand. Most of the other blokes were scared of him and his air of menace kept them all in order. But secretly, Nig was also a very clever boy indeed, a sensitive soul who read James Joyce, came from a broken home on the other side of the tracks at Wealdstone and had attended the notorious Hatch End High. Also on our coach that night was Jamie, the bass player from the now successful band The Cult. They had just had a hit single out and Nig delighted in good naturedly taking the piss out of him throughout the whole journey.

Once at the club, we didn't see much of the band due to having drunk so much on the way. Nig was practically unconscious and Ian wasn't far behind him. He as good as fell into me, then he asked me to hold his hand and from that moment on he was all over me. The trip home was even more fun than the journey up there had been. Ian lay in my lap and Nig leaned over and poured lager on him, so I poured mine on Nig and this is how we amused ourselves in those times. Then Ian nearly got into a fight with some guy (I can't recall why, if we ever did know), but we calmed it down. The coach eventually stopped at Hatch End and I asked Ian if he wanted me to go with him, which he did, so we staggered down the steps with everyone shouting goodbye and banging on the windows as the vehicle drove off. We took a short cut to Ian's through the park by The Boxtree pub. It was a wild and windy October night and the trees were waving and dancing about madly; their sinister branches looked very black against the background of a navy sky. I was practically carrying Ian and he whispered a great many interesting and naughty things into my ear as we made our way along the uneven footpaths to his house, treading on conkers and various bits of flotsam as we went. There the bliss continued, only marred by Ian falling out of that bloody bed in the night and me having a right palaver trying to get him back in again.

A few days later, Zazie rang and said her mother was away, so would Ian and I like to come over that evening and stay there in a double bed? I wasn't sure what Ian would say to this. It was a bit too like being a real boyfriend and girlfriend for him to deal with. He didn't appear at the pub until really late. As I could have predicted, he was fairly cold after Wednesday's excess of affection, but he came back to Zazie's and I was so drunk that the room was spinning. A white room in fact, not far from the station, but with red curtains and a red and white spotted duvet cover on smart pine double bed.

The next day I had to go back to the hospital for my results and I expected to get told off for bonking but the doctor said it looked 'wonderful' and 'as good as new' (result!). Then Ian ran away again and my world collapsed in ruins. By the time of that horrid Scorpions birthday at the very end of October, we were at daggers drawn. Jonah asked me if I would go to Ian's birthday bash at The Warehouse in Camden, but I retorted that I was going nowhere unless he bothered to invite me himself. 'If I left you two alone in a room together you'd kill each other', He sighed, 'all the guy wants is a clean break and you're being stroppy, lairy and ungentle to him.'

They went off to Camden and I went back to a house that was rented by Marlon, my new admirer. He was older and hippy-ish, with long brown hair, a wide jaw and a beard! Not a young, wild hooligan with a messed up head, which was what I hankered after, but I flirted outrageously anyway, hating myself more and more with every false come on that I gave.

'I hope I'm not putting you on a pedestal', he said.

'Please do.' I replied.

'Would you like to go to bed with me now?'

'Pardon?' I laughed, but then I began to think, 'Help!'

Alison Moyet began to sing 'All Cried Out' from the music system and inevitably thoughts of Ian were uppermost in my mind. *'You took a whole lot of loving for a handful of nothing...'* How terribly heavy and painful my heart felt. I wanted to go home so I made my apologies to Marlon and I stumbled towards the front door of the little house that was long ago flattened to make way for the pedestrian underpass at the Roxborough Bridge.

'I think you're wrong, but I will respect you,' he uttered in a tone of faux chivalry.

'Deary me,' thought I, 'I'm not leaving for any noble reasons, if I fancied you, you would have lost your trousers long ago; but there you are.'

I graciously gave him a kiss goodbye, which only

confirmed in my own mind the fact that it would be useless even to go there.

'When will I see you again?' he asked (there's a song about that isn't there?).

But The Three Degrees wearing their spangled dresses did not break into song in my head at this moment, for I merely replied, 'Down the pub sometime,' without the faintest show of enthusiasm.

QOS did a gig up at The Africa Centre in Covent Garden and a load of us went up on the train. Two West Indian geezers came over to me and told me I was wonderfully beautiful and that boosted my ego two million yards out of the roof. All the elite gang were being very kind to me over the Ian business, so it seems that I did present quite a sorry sight. As usual, Big Lisa had to help me home because I was so out of it and we sang Blake's 'Jerusalem' all the way back from the station at the tops of our voices.

*'I will not cease this mental fight, nor shall my sword sleep in my hand'*...

(They played it at her funeral after she had taken her own life in 1991. Her coffin rested there, still and silent as the grim February light filtered down through the high windows of the crematorium.)

...*"til we have built Jerusalem on England's green and pleasant land.'*

Meanwhile, back in the days when we only had a vague presentiment of the disasters that were one day to overtake us, Slimy, Simon, Mitch (who was a dead ringer for Rupert Everett and had a lovely girlfriend named Paula) and a guy named Vince, had formed a new band. They called themselves The Saddlewhores and were doing a gig supporting Alien Sex Fiend up at The Clarendon. We weren't too thrilled at having to pay £4.50 to get in, due to the other band being quite big and the place was packed solid with Goths (whom we derided for some reason). Nevertheless, I got nicely drunk and the band began what was to become their tradition of passing down the amyl nitrate from the stage in order to get us all going. They always played a storming version of 'Greased Lightning' with all the actions and Mitch had a guitar shaped like a machine gun. We really rated them, but perhaps in truth, the drugs, drink and atmosphere made them sound a lot better than they actually were. Of course that was the point of it all anyway and they also produced a T-shirt (designed by Simon who was a talented artist), depicting a half naked woman astride a motorbike and bearing the slogan, *'Amyl nitrate and gasoline, get out my way I'm fucking mean.'*

After they had done their bit, we all trooped back downstairs for a drink as we didn't fancy 'Sex Fiend' that much. I was having a grand time and Pat, the singer from Malice was being very amusing. Also, Adam and I were getting on really well. Off I went to the loos and was happily skipping back up the stairs to the bar, when I came face to face with bloody Ian Chambers, who winked at me. CRASH! My heart fell out of my shoes and that was the end of my good time. I said, 'Hello' very coolly and went to sit in between Adam and Pat for safety, but it all went downhill from there. We had planned to go off to a party at the place of a girl called Little Brigitte, who lived near me. Ian somehow got it into his head that everyone was going to my house first to change into fancy dress, then when he looked over at me with Pat and Adam he began to get aggressive and said he was going home. It took a great effort by Zazie to talk him round and so, unfortunately for me, he stayed. He'd also told Pete that he and I weren't getting on, so at least he'd noticed, but I felt very sad. We went off to get the train and Gaz was trying to drag me along but I was by then hanging back to wait for Ian.

Ian appeared and Gaz only went and told him that I'd wanted to wait for him, which made me feel even worse. On the station steps, Jonah needed a wee and asked me to hold his carrier bag that was filled with drink. But as he passed it over the handles broke and a bottle of Scotch that Tufty and Zazie had given Ian as a birthday present (making me feel bad for not even getting him a card), smashed onto the concrete. We stared dumbly down at the sorry mass of broken glass and spilled brown fluid, streaks of which dashed over the torn label. The stench of whisky filled the air. Ian and I had bad karma when we were together that much was for sure. Jonah went off and found an 'offie' and replaced the bottle and I stuffed all the money I had left into Ian's pocket just to assuage my own guilt. I didn't know what I could give him to make his life better. Obviously, 'nothing' was the answer.

Once on the train, I sat on the floor feeling sorry for myself, and Gaz, who felt sorry for me too, came and sat next to me. After a while, a grubby little hand proffering the bottle of Scotch kept appearing round the corner of the seats. He also kept trying to get me to take my five-pound note back, but I refused and he must have thought that I was mad. At West Harrow, I had to pop home and get my drink and I wanted someone to come with me so Tufty volunteered and he reckoned that Ian gave him a look as we went off. It seems doubtful. At mine, we met up with Big Lisa and we walked around the corner to this party in Dorchester Avenue, where the inevitable happened and Ian and I began talking. I suggested that we sit down and he ended up sprawled all over me and totally crashed out. There is a place for this in the world, however tragic it may appear. I've seen photos of Keith Richards crashed out on Anita Pallenberg (lucky her) and ones of girls happily taking advantage of a practically comatose Johnny Thunders. It does happen and some of us masochistic saddos do like a helpless man, and as I've said before at least they can't run away. Several friends, who thought they occupied the moral high ground and/or were trying to protect me from further heartbreak, came past and told me off. Only Pikes offered me complete understanding. By now, I had begun to feel a bit queasy and had to go outside to throw up, then I came back in and drank some more which made me feel better. After what seemed to me to be like several hours hard work, I managed to get Ian up and say to him, 'Come home.'

He staggered uncertainly down the road to my house with me holding him up and I said, 'Its okay, you can say you were too drunk to remember where you were.'

This provoked a curious reaction in him, because he then started kissing me repeatedly, saying that he was in no state to stay anywhere and that he wanted to go home. The problem was that he was in no state to get home either and I began to worry that he would just collapse in the street somewhere. I should have left him to it, but I insisted and he capitulated. He woke up with a hangover (surprise!) and was late for Mick the Malice drummer's wedding, so I rang a cab for him. 'Thanks for saving me last night'. He said.

On Pete's birthday, we all went down to Tudors for 'Alternative Night.' It was one of those evenings when try as you might you don't seem to be able to get drunk. After five vodkas, two pints of lager and three bottles of Pils I felt quite sober (until I got in). Ian was not there and I got talking to Adam again who walked me home. On the way he practically asked me out and said that he really wanted a girlfriend. Now what you may ask yourself was wrong with him? And I asked myself the very same question a million times. He was young, Punky, a bit unhappy, tattoos, tall and safe, loving and kind. Yet somehow, 'no' and I can't tell you why. I saw Ian again as soon as I walked into Bumbles Wine Bar a few nights later for a Malice gig. My heart flew out of its socket, my legs turned to jelly and my knees disappeared into another dimension. He looked quite pleased to see me, but later I thought that I may have imagined this. He sidled over and thanked me for the other night, whilst I just swooned and said it was, 'okay.' He said he'd got some speed and would I like some? Jonah came along and was a bit off with me to start with, but by the end of the evening he'd proposed to me twice.

'Why do you keep going off with Ian?' he asked me

'Either I'm in love, or I'm very ill,' was my reply.

At the end of the band's set Ian got up and stood in with them. He looked like more of a geezer than ever and it certainly did nothing to lessen my hero worship of him, quite the reverse. I decided to resign myself to the fact that I loved him but would never get him and would have to be alone for eternity as a consequence. When he came off stage I kissed him. He gave me one of the many drinks that he had lined up at the bar in front of him. Then he kissed me when we met outside the toilets. The speed made me feel much better, quite benevolent and good natured and I thought that if Ian couldn't make me happy himself, then at least he was able to provide me with something that did the job just as well. When he left, I beckoned him over and asked him to call me.

Time went on and I have to say that I had quite a few nice chaps interested in me. Adam thought he had a chance and Pat began to walk me home from the pub on a regular basis. He always had me falling on the ground with laughter and really was the most entertaining and intelligent bloke you could ever hope to meet. He wasn't unattractive either, but Pat never said one thing to indicate that he liked me in that way and it wasn't until many years later that I realised that he might possibly have done so. He was lovely, but it never even crossed my mind. Then there was Marlon and some other bods, not forgetting Tim and his great walking home service. But even with all this support I sat in a corner of the pub crying because I missed Ian so much. I knew that he didn't want me and that he still loved Dolly bloody Mixture, but understanding the bald truth of it couldn't stop the way I felt. How annoying.

Then things livened up slightly. Gaz and Pat made real efforts to cheer me up at the pub and then we went off to a party at that same house as I'd carried Ian home from previously. Sandra told me that Marlon had been banging on about me endlessly and had even shaved off his beard. Sigh. Indeed I could still see many of them flying over my head. Ian was avoiding me thank God and I told myself that I couldn't have everything my own way and I needed to get over it. The party was quite lively for a change, with people up and dancing. Adam had been 'off' with me at the pub, but now he came over and offered me some speed and I said 'no,' because I'd decided that I wanted to get to sleep at some point. He was a bit sad and went off. As I cast my eyes about with that sick realisation that I had, in fact, exhausted all my stock, my gaze alighted happily upon Tris's brother Steve. I thought he may ignore me after all the hoo ha that had gone on with Tris and I, but no, he sauntered over and was jolly friendly indeed. He did talk about his brother quite a lot and I felt as though I couldn't have cared less about Tris at that moment. I also spoke to Peg who said, 'why can't I get a girlfriend?' and to

Pat who asked me the same question.

Then I got the terrible hiccups and had to go into the kitchen to cure them. In the doorway stood Marlon and another bod. 'Marlon will help you with your hiccups,' said the bod, and I slapped him round the face (not hard).

I kept popping back to the dancing room where Steve was. He wouldn't let me sit down and I was telling him how much I liked him. I began to get a bit wobbly and decided that it was home time, so I went over to Steve to say goodbye and we got into a very long kiss. Oh woe, that he never liked me, because I knew again his intelligence, his tall beauty and his soothing voice. Out of my league though, a long way out. The pain of Ian had not gone, but thanks to Steve I felt a lot better. So I tripped off home, with Marlon's eyes boring into me from the kitchen doorway as I went.

On a very wet Monday in November we had a little party at Zola's mum's lovely new cottage high up on Harrow Hill. It was a tiny place and you had to go up a ladder to get to Zola's bedroom, which was up in the roof space. We got very out of it just for a change and Zola's mum, who was about forty-three, got off with this twenty-six year old bloke that we knew, and as far as I know they are still together now. I mention this because it was another incident that gave me hope for the future and made me realise that life doesn't end after twenty-five. This was just as well, because for me, twenty-six was rapidly approaching, what a ghastly thought and then only four years 'til thirty. Then I reminded myself that Joan Collins was still doing okay at fifty-two, so maybe I had a few more years yet? That night Zola gave me so much vodka that I was practically unconscious and in fact must have actually been so, as I never noticed the other party goers leave and they would have had to walk right over my head to get to the front door. We spent the morning being nasty about Mr Pig and I realised that Ian and Tris's 'Hog Gang' had well and truly scattered since I had come along. You can always rely on a woman to ruin everything.

November wore on; the parks were strewn with soggy leaves and twigs that had been stripped off the wet branches by the wind, floated aimlessly about in the puddles. For the time being, 'Punk World' still continued on apace, Pinz came round and we played 'bleaching our hair'. Then the long lost Duncan turned up before heading off to the studios at Acton to see my siblings, where he made an amusing video. In this they pretended to sniff glue out of one of those 'gummy' bottles of paper adhesive to a sound track of Motörhead's 'Ace of Spades.' Down at The Beard I was still holding forth. '*…and don't forget the joker.*'

There I stood, dressed in black, at the centre of my own little scene, basking in attention. Marlon looked longingly at me, then approached me tentatively and said, 'I'm sorry if I bothered you at that party.'

Three other lads that I knew were dancing attendance and Pat asked to walk me home. Then Tris appeared and started to be very bitchy and I guessed that he had got wind of the incident with Steve. I went and wrote 'Dolly and Bee are better than me' in big letters in the condensation on the window. Gorgeous Gaz came over with a drink for me and then he told me that Ian and Dolly were definitely an item again and I wished that he hadn't said it. Peg came home with me with bad intent and he moaned all the way about how lonely he was. What a shame, my heart bleeds. When we got in, I had to make him toast (resentment), then he grabbed me and was getting really passionate and I was thinking, 'Ho hum, I'm not into this at all.'

How could I ever have liked him so much? I felt rather like an interested spectator, all technique and no feeling and I got a bit cross with my stupid body, which had craved intimacy for so long and I had said to it, 'Here you are then' and it replied, 'but not this one, this isn't the one we like.' So I say, 'tough shit, this is all I could get for you today', but it still didn't work.

My God, it was bad, but at the same time it was rather hilarious and he looked so funny that I could have burst out laughing. Oh deary me, he was so keen and totally different from times gone by. He was very relaxed and he wanted to stay and go to sleep. A great torrent of anger welled up inside of me and it was all I could do to restrain myself from smashing everything in sight into pieces. I asked him to leave. Peg was aghast and very humpy and hurt. 'Now you know how it feels.' I said, filled with the triumphant spite of revenge served cold.

Though in reality I know that I only hurt myself and when he left I thought about Ian and turned up the tape player...

*'I bet you wonder how I knew*
*you were gonna make me blue*
*with some other [girl] you knew before*
*out of the two of us both you know I love you more*
*[...] If you love somebody else*
*Why couldn't you tell me yourself?*
*Instead I heard it through the grapevine*
*Not much longer would you be mine,*
*Yes I heard it through the grapevine*
*And I'm just about to lose my mind...'*
('I Heard It Through The Grapevine', Marvin Gaye)

Big Lisa and I got the train up to The Electric Ballroom in Camden Town for another gig of QOS's. The place was practically empty, a case of, '*Who let the dog in for free?*' (The Comic Strip TV show: *Bad News On Tour*).

For some reason (and I think that Special Brew had something to do with it), I got totally and utterly smashed, so much so that I could hardly speak. We got a lift back from QOS's and I had to keep my eyes shut all the way as usual to avoid throwing up. Then I woke up with the massive headache that only Special Brew can give you.

On the last weekend in November 1986, I had to do five hours nude at the college and I nearly fainted about three times. I was not enjoying it, but I needed the dosh. Then we all went up to see The Saddlewhores play at The Clarendon and luckily for me Ian wasn't there and Nig was, which was a pleasant distraction. At The Clarendon, there was loads of Amyl zooming about and we were all down at the front rucking, when QOS's elbow connected with my mouth and blood flew everywhere. Afterwards, I didn't want to go home so we all went back to a squat in Shepherds Bush, where Nig, Tufty, Pongo, Pinner and Simon were living. It cheered me up to be having a bit of an 'adventure' and to go to a place that I'd never been to before, even if it was only a cold and empty flat on The White City Estate. When we arrived there, Nig was acting like the perfect gentleman and this amazed me after all the bad things I'd heard about him. We began to talk about the birthday party I'd decided to throw up at The Pumphouse in Watford and Pinner and Pongo mentioned in passing that they'd heard Ian say he wouldn't be turning up because I didn't like him. This played on my mind as Zazie, Tufty, Zola and I all crammed into Nig's bed, though it was a shame that he wasn't in it too (who said that?). So, the next day I very foolishly indeed rang

Ian to say, 'what's going on?'

He sounded very pleased to hear from me and he was quite crawly. He said that he didn't think I'd want to see him at my party and I told him not to be so stupid. However, he conveniently forgot to mention the reason why I might not want him there and therein lies the rub. He said he would see me at the pub that evening and false hope flooded through me. I got all jittery and elated after that, thinking, 'I'm going to see him at last,' and all that crap.

Once there, sure enough I spotted him strolling along through the broken townscape with Midget and Jonah. He looked wonderfully dishevelled, whilst behind him hung the backdrop of the half demolished shops and the rusty scaffolding poles against the brittle sparkle of new plate glass. My heart flew away as they came straight over to our table. But then a voice chirps up from out of the fug of smoke behind us, 'Oh, hello Ian dear, I have come to meet you', and its Dolly.

It quickly became clear to me that they were indeed back together. It's not as if I hadn't been told of it a million times, but for some unexplained reason, I obviously was unable to fully comprehend the fact until it was waved about right under my nose. In the light of this, Ian got conveniently plastered and was incoherent and falling all over the place, but he was also all over Dolly when my back was turned. I told him not to bring her to my party and he said, 'That's cool.' Suddenly, Dolly turned to me and waved, 'Hello Nettie.' My jaw hit the floor.

'Look, I really don't feel like being nice to you,' I said coldly.

A few drinks and more emotional agitation later she got Ian to kiss her in front of me. For a moment the world paused and then I went berserk. I grabbed poor Ian by the hair and shouted, 'Fuck this!'

Then I turned round and threw my glass into the air, drenching the crowd with cider. They all parted like The Red Sea before me as I shouted, 'fuck this!' again and stormed out into the darkness kicking everything I could see and repeatedly saying, 'fuck'.

Oh what a marvellous vocabulary this girl has. Opposite the pub, the old Adam's furniture store lay in shattered ruins as if it were a bombsite. I went and sat on a plank amid the broken shards of the mirrors that had once adorned the outside wall of the store. Jap and I used to laugh at our reflections in them as we passed by, in the far off days when we bought our Biba nail varnish and talked about boys; so full of hope for the future in our pleasant little town. The shining romance of Punkdom had begun to tarnish. The sound of running feet was not long in coming. Sandra and Pinz were first on the scene, followed closely by dear Simon. He kept kissing me and telling me that I was wonderful as far as he was concerned. What a great guy for being so kind to an old drama queen like me. Others appeared shortly bearing the gifts of kind words and I saw Jonah leaving in a distraught state. Dolly disappeared and Ian just sat there swaying with a very drunken and smug smile upon his face. He probably thought he was great with two women fighting for his body. What he really thought, no one now knows or cares I shouldn't think. So Sandra drove me home, where I took eight aspirins and hoped I'd never wake up, which of course I did.

# CHAPTER TWELVE
## 1987: Bad Company

The winter wind in the freezing street,
Racing litter and hurrying feet,
Seedy stairways, a lone dog's cry,
Through a broken window, a snow filled sky.

Shards of glass and rusty tins,
Contents of the world's rubbish bins,
Used up needles, fag ends glow,
Showering ash in the wind, they blow.

Punks at the bus stop, backs to the cold,
Gob in the gutter; don't like to be told.
From Shepherds Bush tube
Scuffed boots tramp the pavements.
Swig homemade wine.
Take speed in damp basements.
Bleak granite steps, stilettos ring,
To a smashed up flat
Where the drunk boys sing.

Late night a party, rooms glowing red,
Snogging a glue sniffer out of your head.
The boys storm the stairwell, trouble outside
With axe-wielding Skinheads;
The Pigs have arrived.

Raw winds of winter,
Times of some pity,
Can you remember
The squats at White City?

Well folks, here we are on the very last chapter you'll be glad to know. The ultimate contrast between what had been for me the sunny, moneyed Seventies and the grey, grim poverty-stricken Eighties was about to be attained. Without a doubt Punk, or this latest incarnation of it, had given me something of value, but metaphorically speaking the air at the top of that particular pinnacle of achievement had become a little too rare to breathe now without incurring some lasting physical damage. Our little town was changing just as much as the youths who grew up in it and even the sacred Royal Beard itself was now under the builders hammer. For months we were crammed into various small areas of the bar until eventually the whole of our cosy little section was closed off, causing it to be renamed (by us), 'The Half Beard'. Then the cordons were removed and we were presented with a vast, impersonal and echoing space, consisting of high, piddling, round mahogany tables sporting glass tops and with flashing chrome bars curving around them. Now it was a Yuppy pub and it soon became clear that the likes of us were not the clientèle that they hoped to encourage. The Royal Beard (Oak) then emerged as a tiny soulless place whose name changes by the hour, plonked unceremoniously like a doll's house hard against the giant buildings that have risen up menacingly in the middle of the boring and pedestrianised town centre. The spot where Adam's furniture store had been was briefly grassed over and for a spell we'd sit and drink there on summer nights, enjoying the ambience of 'The Grassy Knoll' as we called it. But soon that too was bulldozed flat, to make way for the sprawling abomination that is now St George's shopping centre.

But in December 1986, my twenty-sixth birthday party

was fast approaching and Sandra printed up the tickets for me. I was charging £1 a head in order to cover the hire of the place and they sold well. I hadn't invited Tris, Bee, Dolly and Ian for obvious reasons and I hoped that they might go and have their own private incendiary bomb party some place else. Zola said I was going soft and forced me to drink Holsten and wear a paper beard. QOS's band got into the finals of a 'Battle of the Bands' style competition and I went with Big Lisa to The Riverside Studios in Hammersmith to see them do their thing. I thought that the other bands were really boring, badly done Jazz Funk stuff and I felt that QOS's lot were far too spirit of '77 for the judges to cope with at that time. The ideal of aggression had faded out in the 'Feed the World' political climate of '86.

Bad dreams continued along with the winter weather, as the Ian and Dolly saga played itself out night after night in my fevered brain, but ever the optimist, I was determined to push on like the hero that I am. This was helped by the fact that my Nanny and Grandad had very kindly sent me £40 for Christmas and perhaps I shouldn't tell you that I spent it all on alcohol and amphetamine sulphate. Zola and I then went to the pub and hooked up with Pinz, Tim, Peg and several others. We were having quite a lively time of it, but unfortunately there were some beer boy types in there being very obnoxious who began to piss us right off. Zola ended up shouting at them and when we left they were waiting for us in the car park that was situated where the buses now stop outside St George's. Our guys were all carrying bottles, including some unknown blokes who had kindly joined in on our side and Tim quickly smashed his in order to make a handy weapon. Thankfully, we managed to get home without a fight and Tim made me laugh by showing me that his bottle had in fact broken so high up the neck that he was practically left holding the lid!

A few nights later, Both Ian and Tris were at The Beard, without their usual appendages of Carpet-head and Dolly Mixture. Tris cut a lonely figure at the bar and kept casting sad looks in my direction, but Ian on the other hand, came in all guns blazing and intent upon my destruction. 'Are you not talking to me now?' I asked lamely. 'I'd rather not.' Fair enough, straight and to the point, but anger towards him burned low in my heart, eating away at me like a canker.

Ian decided to flirt with Chewing Gum Pauline as much as he could and she was thrilled as well she might have been. However, all was not lost that evening, because there was still someone whose heart was soft where Ian's was like granite. Tris knew I was having a bad time and soon we were talking ten to the dozen like the long lost friends we were. He ended up walking me home, which no doubt provided excellent gossip for everyone and the saga limped on for a bit longer. We stopped about three times on the way just shouting at each other, I admitted that I'd used him to get closer to Ian and he admitted that he'd been jealous, whilst at the same time telling me that he would never leave Bee. 'I asked you wait two days after I finished with her the last time, but you wouldn't!' He said, 'That's a lie!'

'Well, if you hadn't gone off with Ian, we'd be together now.'

'That's a lie! It's easy to say that now, but you would never have made up your mind.'

'Bee is safe and committed to me, you are too popular and I'd be scared to lose you.'

We laughed a lot as well though and amazingly, we got on famously, just as we always had.

The next night Mikki had a party at her flat in Putney. I took two Dexedrine, met QOS and Bondy at Harrow Met and we got the train to Putney Bridge. I was speeding my nuts off and it was a bitterly cold December evening. The freezing flat was full of wallies and the party itself was fairly naff, but I began feeling quite happy and I went on to drink two litres of cider. Then I got in a very strange mood (can't imagine why?) and went and sat alone in a chair most of the night, wishing to speak to no one. QOS was being mean to Bondy, because Little Tris was after her like mad and she was lapping up the flattery. Consequently, Mikki started to get quietly upset (a new concept for me) and it was all getting rather desperate and edgy. Tris and Bee were there and he kept waving at me and then bounded over to give me tickets to a gig of his on the twenty-second. 'Bring the family,' he said cheerfully.

I went into the kitchen where he was and Bee stood in a corner talking to another soul. Tris was messing about with a large carving knife and was photographed with it clamped between his teeth, but then he sprang at me, held the cold steel to my throat and said, 'I hate you!' Adding, 'Not really, everything I said last night still stands.'

'Great! One minute you hate me, then the next you love me.'

'Now you are back in my life I can't think straight.' He answered despairingly.

Oh no, here goes the old Drama Queen again. He came to find me in the other room and things were back to how they'd always been, with him molesting me when Bee's back was turned, but this wasn't at all what I had had in mind. I gave him a quarter of an inch and he took fifty miles, all in the space of twenty-four hours, but that my dears, is the nature of the beast. He said he'd told Bee that he'd made it up with me and predictably her reply was that she'd rather we still hated each other and I couldn't say I blamed her. He continued kissing and hugging me and said, 'what have you done to me? Bee is afraid that you will take me away from her, but I said there is no chance of that.'

'Thanks a lot.'

Then he disappeared with a large bowl of tomatoes. QOS's drummer (not another one) came over to see me in my lonely chair and started kissing my stockings (he was like that with everyone). Suddenly a tomato, which had been expertly aimed at this poor guy, came flying through the air and splatted to the floor. The jealous Harem master strikes again. I wanted to go home and so did poor Bondy, but QOS was enjoying herself immensely and was having none of it. So Bondy, the other drummer and I, hid miserably in a corner 'til Tris came over and said farewell to Bondy and to the drummer geezer, then leaned over, kissed me passionately and was gone.

'He didn't really want to say goodbye to me,' said the drummer, 'he just used that as an excuse to kiss you.'

'I know.'

The main thing that seems to have upset Tris was that his friendship with Ian had gone down the tubes and that had only happened since I had come along. So when I got home I sat down and wrote a seasonal letter to Ian, saying that at this time of year we should all forgive each other, that everything was my fault and that even if he never spoke to me again, would he consider lowering his pride and make it up with Tris. It was worth a try at least and was my own futile attempt to throw a rope bridge across the yawning cavern of enmity that I had unwittingly created between them.

At last, the day of my party was nearly upon us and suddenly I found that I needed to borrow fifty quid cash for the deposit and quick as a flash QOS was on my doorstep with the readies. The big day arrived and I had reached a grand old age. Gifts consisted of a Ghetto Blaster, silver hoop earrings and some Oil of Ulay to keep the wrinkles at bay. The party was styled as 'Wild West' fancy dress and I went as a bar room floozy (not typecast or anything) with black corset, fishnet stockings, frilly petticoat, lace up boots and feathers in my hair. Quite a few others made a concerted effort, including Peg who came dressed as a Native American Chief and what with his long black hair and large hooked nose he looked very impressive indeed. Before we left home, Zola had asked me why I was taking two huge empty carrier bags with me and I answered, 'For the presents.' 'You won't need them.' Was her reply, but by the end of the night they were full to bursting!

It was a fiasco to begin with, as we had to wait ages for the bar staff to arrive, then Seamus's band couldn't get hold of a van to get their equipment there and as all the other bands had planned on using it as well it was a bit unfortunate. But in the end Nig, Tufty and Pinner saved the day by constructing a drum kit out of various beer barrels, a snare and some cymbals, then The Saddlewhores took to the stage, passed down the amyl and we were off. Friends appeared from far and wide and even Alan and Gayle from Chalfont turned up. Everyone had a good time. QOS was sick on Bondy's feet and I got bombed on Dexedrine and vodka. I had to go and be violently sick in the middle, but then I felt better and continued drinking and dancing. Simon then presented me with a whole load more whizz and the wonderful Nig was acting the star and began to make a big impression upon me. The night ended back at mine, with me dancing on the old dining room table and several very handsome young men all crashing out with me in my bedroom!

Time having its skates on as usual, rapidly presented us with yet another Christmas Eve and it was hard to believe that a whole year had passed since the creepy Richard boy from Newcastle had so got on my nerves. Firstly, I joined Mum down at the Neasden wine bar, where I imbibed six or seven double vodkas and her male colleagues plied me with gifts of cigarettes and money. By eight thirty p.m. Zola and I were up The Beard and the place was buzzing as never before. There was a fun fight involving spray string and Adam accidentally set my hair on fire with a lighted match. Then we got pelted with rubber Johnnies filled with water and covered with shaving foam, most of which ended up in my drink. Nig asked me to kiss him, so I did right there in the middle of the bar, with broken glass and beer everywhere. Apparently we all got barred, but I don't think that anybody realised!

On Christmas afternoon we had the usual onslaught, plus Pinz just in time for her traditional green pint. We watched the episode of Eastenders in which Arthur Fowler has embezzled the Christmas club money and has a breakdown. This dramatic moment in Soap-land prompted Nig to lead us all in a rousing rendition of 'Arthur is a cabbage' at the tops of our lungs. Zazie had earlier confided in me that Nig didn't get off with girls because his heart belonged to a wild and dark-eyed young trouble maker named Sima (or however you spell it). Of course that was like a red rag to a bull to me. Nig had by now crashed out in the dining room comatose and was lolling in one of the high backed nineteenth-century chairs. His well-muscled arms rested on his strong lean legs and his noble, ginger head nodded over his lap. Momentarily, the room emptied and a hush ensued. At this point warning lights should have been flashing and klaxons sounding to alert a poor, unwary and severely weakened prey that a dangerous predator was on the loose. I went and sat at his feet, 'Nig are you okay?' I asked softly. We went to bed.

Yes, me and the man that Zazie said didn't get off with people. In fact the actual deed did not happen, not because he was incapable (I can assure you that that was not the case), but because of his love for that aforementioned girl. But he was very sweet to me and it was a source of lasting regret that I never did get anything else together with him. But once again he was too cool, too in demand and too out of my league for me to get a look in. He did say that he would like people to think he was different and yes, he was. He possessed dignity, he had integrity and he was as scary as fuck!

Sadly, on Boxing Day, the ginger vision went off to see the love of his life and so that, as they say, was the end of that. New Year's Eve arrived and I felt that it echoed the emptiness that can only be achieved when you drink and drug and do naughty things too much and to no discernible gain. Zola and I went to the pub and I wore a skin-tight dark blue satin fishtail dress that Stripey Jayne had made for me. I still had some of the whizz that Simon had given me for my birthday (which I thought was very economical of me), so I took that and remembered the previous year's debacle when I'd ended up with Foundation Face in my bed. There was a party afterwards at Mitch and Paula's gaff in Watford, so we went along there. Firstly, I made a complete tit of myself by singing 'Diamonds Are A Girl's Best Friend' in my Monroe dress and I'm sure they all cringed with embarrassment for me, because I do even now whenever I think of it. After that I passed the time by looking at myself in the mirror, whilst Zola ate all the sandwiches. The party guests were mainly couples and it got very depressing. Pat was there, but as you already know, I wasn't a bit interested in him. Some unidentified guy fell asleep and we plastered him in make-up, then Zola and I got a cab home for an extortionate price in the pouring rain. Welcome to 1987.

Two nights later, I was in the pub when Ian walked in alone and as usual, I felt the bones in my thighs empty of marrow and fill with water. Eventually when enough alcohol had been consumed, we broke the deadlock and he told me that I had given him his first bad trip and that Dolly's ex boyfriend had sent two heavies round armed with golf clubs, to beat him up (with some difficulty I kept myself from laughing). Not unusually for me, I was short on sympathy for my own little Devil. Nevertheless, Zola and I took him and Midget back to my place, where we smoked dope whilst the two boys talked about running off to Canada to shoot the rapids and we took the piss out of them unmercifully. They reckoned that they were going to fly out there in two year's time, but we laughed so much that they cut it to six months. They had no idea about the realities of getting visas with criminal convictions, work permits, how long you're allowed to stay, money you'd need etc. They really believed that they could go and build a shack in the woods and live on rabbits, when Ian even hated the mud at Reading. Imagine a frozen winter, with no pub... and bears! Midget said he had a relative out there, so we thought it more likely that they'd sponge off them and then Ian mentioned going off down the white water in his canoe, when he'd only ever paddled one around Ruislip Lido before. He said he just wanted to get away from the 'hassle' of Dolly and I (he maintained they were still together, but Midget told me that they weren't). God did we laugh and said things like, 'I'll believe it when I see it,' and 'I really hope you do it.'

When I asked, 'What about sex?' they replied that they

would visit a whorehouse once a month. Well, that's about how often they thought about it and what would they pay with? Buttons? Annie Lennox was singing 'The Miracle of Love' from my new tape player and Zola began to cry softly about Mr Pig. Ian was shocked when I told him about Nig and I on Christmas Night and he told me that he'd received my letter regarding Tris but that he still didn't like him. However, *'the miracle of love'* did manage to take away my pain for me for one last time. The other two disappeared, 'Have you missed me?' I asked when we kissed. 'I missed your love' came the reply, with the stress on that last word. When he fell asleep he snored and muttered and I stuck my tongue out at him. In the morning we were more antagonistic with each other than ever. Still, at very least I'd got one over on that smug cow Dolly.

The world froze up and snow flurries whirled around the suburban streets. The sea froze off the Essex coast and so did our pipes, which caused the dishwasher to spew water all over the kitchen. Snow blew in under the conservatory door, giving us a mini drift in the house and a force ten gale began to blow with a wind chill of minus fourteen. A woman from the Art College kept phoning and hassling me to go and get naked in the sub zero temperature. I was starting to get fed up with this posing lark and it wasn't too long before I knocked it on the head. I took the very last of my speed and met up with Zola, Janet, Pete, Adam and Janet's brother at South Harrow. We got the train to Ealing Common and breezed into Bumbles, where joy of joys, Nig was holding court again. We chatted quite a bit, but I soon became aware that there were millions of women after him. Hig was there too, acting as our very own 'Del boy' (though he looked more like 'Sick Boy' from *Trainspotting*), trying to sell us all dodgy watches and other similar knocked off items that he had hanging up inside his jacket like a wartime Spiv. Eventually, I found myself on a Routemaster bus with Nig, Simon and Pinner. Nig and I took it in turns to wear a peaked, Bus Driver's type hat of his as we travelled along on an anarchic, jolting journey that brought us back to the urban squalor of The White City estate. A lot of the apartments here had been boarded up and/or smashed up to deter squatters, obviously not to much effect. The boys were always handily equipped with crowbars and jemmies and were constantly on the look out for new places to stay. It was normally Pongo, Simon, Tufty and Pinner who lived together, with Nig acting as their Commander in Chief. He had quite a fatherly influence over them but he wouldn't think twice about fighting to keep the status quo. We had a good time that night until one of Nig's fan club turned up and went and got into his bed, so Zola and I slept with Pongo.

Now Pongo was two years younger than everybody else, so that made him seven years my junior. He was a good six foot two in height and big built, with a boyish face and dark blonde hair and he modelled himself on Nig. That also meant that he was looking for a girl to fall in love with and to whom he could be devoted. He gave off that same air of safety that Tris possessed and I shouldn't say this really because they later came to hate each other with a passion, but sorry guys, there were similarities. All the other sub-gangs however, definitely looked upon Pongo 'the speed freak' as a bit infra dig and as a callow youth who wasn't quite up to cool. Nevertheless, there I was squashed up to big safe Pongo and as it was me, some kissing happened. I didn't get any sleep and I became rather embarrassed in the light of day. We all felt like death and Zola was being hassled unmercifully by some random black guy so she wanted to leave. My stomach hurt and my head felt like it had been split with a meat cleaver as we struggled through the snow, dishevelled and hung over, slipping on the icy pavements that led us down to Shepherds Bush tube, with Zola's new admirer hot upon our heels.

Feeling dismal I later went off to a Saddlewhores gig that it took ages to get to because the trains were up the spout. It was in a dingy place full of weirdies and we had some Amyl, but then the band got barred for throwing their mics about.

*'Band won't play no more*
*too much fighting on the dance floor.'*
('Ghost Town', The Specials)

Mr Pig turned up, so Zola wept. Then she went bonkers and I had trouble even getting her on a train. I kept losing her and she became convinced that I didn't like her and kept saying that she thought she was dead. Gordon Bennett! We stopped at Acton Town and Mr Pig got on. I could tell straight away that he thought, 'Oh no,' and I went and sat on the other side of the carriage in the right hump. It's a hard world out there.

I went on a disastrous coach trip, where there was no one hunky at all and I had to suffer Tris and Bee. At first he was quite nice and I liked him again but after a while he began to drive me bats. He started moaning on about Ian again, though why they were still bothering with it now that I was off the scene I had no idea. The club was filled with anarchic/hippy types and had quite a decent atmosphere, but then Mr Pig decided that he thought I was marvellous. Ugh, for a start; and help, for a second because I didn't want that happening in front of Zola. Was he mad? Was he dim? On the way home he thought he was coming back with me and even Zola noticed, it was awful and embarrassing. Shortly afterwards, Zola and I were in the pub when who should walk in but Pongo. I was standing by the loos and noticed his tactical manoeuvres to get over to me, so I rushed into the toilets and when I came out, there he was talking to Zola. I could tell that he was having a bit of a swoon over me and it was most gratifying. He asked me if I was going to Seamus's gig up at Dingwalls, which I was and then he invited me about a zillion times to some party they were having up at the squat.

'If you don't come I'll throw things at you.' He said.

'But I've got no money.'

'I'll have my Giro so don't worry about that. Now say definitely yes or no, so that I can wait in for you.' Cripes! It had been about a hundred years since anyone had shown such keenness towards me and you know, he really wasn't that bad.

However, the next day I went off horse riding for the first time in ages. Some young punky sisters who hung out down the pub had a horse and pony over in Stanmore and they persuaded me to go along. Of course I showed off like mad and they were impressed. 'When you said you could ride, we didn't realise you meant you could ride!' They said.

Unfortunately, I forgot the strain it takes on the hamstrings and I couldn't walk for about four days afterwards. In fact I was so crippled that I gave the squat party a miss and let poor Pongo down, which wasn't very nice of me. However, on the first Wednesday in February we were off to Dingwalls for the evening. Zola and I had been too skint to get any speed, so we started on our latest trend, which was to imbibe a combination of lager and vast quantities of either 'Do Do's' or 'Pro-Plus'. These were caffeine based, over the counter 'wake you up' remedies and we found that if you O.d'd on these you got quite a pleasant buzz. So we set off on the bus, stuffing these pills into our gobs with gusto and got the northern line train from Edgware up to Camden Town.

When we arrived at Dingwalls, there were no other Harrow people there, except for a stray barman from The Royal Beard who bought us a drink. Then the rest of the crew and the band turned up and we sat drinking with them. Who else should appear, but Pongo once more, so I awarded him ten points and a gold star for that. Once Mr Pig realised that I was with someone, he started to hover about and sit at our table. Then he offered Zola and I a lift home in the bandwagon. But when they went to leave, Pongo didn't want to go and he asked me to stay with him. I thought this was a grand idea as I was enjoying his company and he was plying me with drinks. I told the others to push off and said I'd be fine with Pongo. Mr Pig came up to me, tried to kiss me and said, 'You're wasting yourself.' A statement that I found to be both hilarious (would he be any better?) and quite frankly, a bloody cheek. Then Seamus rushed over and exclaimed, 'I'm not leaving here without you Nettie!'

I didn't know why they were suddenly acting like my nursemaids, but I told them in no uncertain terms to bog off, because I was having a drink, was perfectly okay and at twenty-six years old was more than capable of deciding what I wanted to do (obviously this is debatable). Off they all went, leaving me with Pongo and it was very exciting and liberating indeed. We walked for miles hand in hand around Trafalgar Square, trying to find the stop for the N18. He even paid my bus fare, then told me off for talking about Ian all the time, adding that Dolly's ex had decked

Ian three times the previous week (a bit unfair really as he was about ten foot taller than poor Ian). Pongo stayed at mine and we laughed a lot. Then the next day I walked him up to West Harrow station, where he gave me a big kiss and said, 'See you later sometime.' Oh no, not those bloody words again. A strange look must have passed across my face because he added, 'I don't know when, but when I can afford to come down again,' which mollified me slightly.

Once more, Zola and I hit The Incredible Shrinking Pub and I walked slap bang into Ian. I had a minor cardiac arrest and we managed to say, 'Hello' to each other. He'd cut off all his beautiful hair and he had funny lace-up shoes on which was a bit upsetting; but I still had a terrible pain in my heart. He seemed to be hanging about like a spare part by himself, but then old Pauline slaggy-face appeared and sure enough she was over in two seconds flat and dragged him away. Dolly was nowhere to be seen, but apparently was still doing the rounds of all her exes for reasons best known to herself. Ian's beady eyes kept boring into me through the throng and I prayed that it wouldn't be too long before I was cured. Ian continued to be seen about with Pauline and I clearly was not at all over it and frequently felt like smashing her stupid little face in. I was madly jealous and oh, if only I could have been blonde and pretty like her then everything would have been different. I suffered so badly in the pub one night, that old Peg said he wanted to hit Ian and Zola grabbed my umbrella and danced outside over the tabletops whilst singing the refrain, 'Nettie is marvellous'. Then we went up to her cottage at the top of Hobbiton to drink copious amounts of vodka. Her mother came in to me and told me to go and look out of her bedroom window and when I did so, there was Zola continuing to sing my praises whilst dancing up and down

Crown Street with my umbrella in the rain.

We were starting to get pissed off with having to frequent a pub the size of a walnut, so Zazie led a contingent that visited The Roxborough again more often. Changes were definitely happening all around us and even QOS had succumbed to council pressure and moved to a flat down in Wealdstone. Her pretty suburban villa now stood disconsolately waiting for the end in the deserted winter street, with windows that had seen better days blinded and boarded up. The march of progress was upon us and soon we were to be trampled asunder in the wake of its relentless jackbooted feet.

On my sister's birthday, 20th February, I got woken up at the ungodly hour of quarter past ten a.m. by the phone and it was Pongo. There was a lot of shouting and hallooing in the background and he jokingly informed me that Nig was in love with me. Yes, I believe you (nice thought though). He said that they were having yet another party up at the squat that very night and that he would meet me at Shepherds Bush tube at eleven. Zola took me out for a pizza first and I was so excited about the coming evening that I drank two bottles of wine and my stomach said, 'help.' Around ten we buggered off up to Shepherds Bush where Pongo met us and he said that he didn't really think that I would turn up because I was 'unreliable.' As we tramped along the frosty pavements and turned into the gloomy back streets, he admitted that it wasn't really a big party and more like a little get together, but he had thought that it was a good excuse to get me there. Then we passed through a dank brick built archway, and entered the run down White City Estate. We went up several flights of hard and sparkling granite steps and the metal tips of my Ad Hoc stilettos rang loudly in the enclosed space. Deafening music came from the doorway of an abandoned flat and that signalled the squat crowd's latest temporary domain.

As usual things were pretty smashed up inside. The main room was lit with dim red bulbs, old mattresses were scattered about the floor and the walls were tastefully decorated with gobbets of solidified green phlegm at strategic intervals. Pongo and I got stuck into each other quite literally as he reeked of the glue he'd been sniffing, some of which was smeared fetchingly across the front of his T-shirt. A bunch of decidedly unfriendly skinheads briefly shattered our peace by running up the stairwell shouting obscenities, brandishing axes and promising death to us all for no immediately identifiable reason. This culminated in an ugly stand off and the Police arrived, but just as soon everyone buggered off again. We went for a nocturnal stroll and some of the lads played chicken with the fast flowing traffic on the A40, though Pongo strongly forbade me from doing so. *[Over eighteen years later, in May 2005, I'd just been to Ahmet Ertegun's after show party in Kensington Palace Gardens, for the Cream reunion at the Royal Albert Hall. Whilst there, I had half heartedly sipped champagne in an elaborately decorated mansion alongside well-dressed A to Z list celebrities, whilst dead lobsters had marched in a surreal fashion over the buffet and the cisterns in the poncy Portaloos outside were covered with a fine layer of white powder. I had chatted amiably with Ginger Baker fan Tom Hanks and other big stars. At four in the morning, I was being taken home in a chauffeur-driven limo. As we purred noiselessly down the old Westway, past White City, I could clearly see our ragged, carefree ghosts of '87, running pell mell along the crash barriers and whooping with delight. I ached to be back there.]*

Whilst I was at the squats, I believed that I was still going somewhere and was about to be off on yet another adventure with The White City crew. Tris rang me out of the blue and expressed some concern because he thought I was getting in with, 'bad company' (*I can't deny it*). But the lure of pastures new had got to me and a couple of days later, I borrowed a fiver, cadged a bottle of homemade wine off Grandma and very bravely got the train up to the squat to surprise Pongo. On the train, I swigged from the bottle to give me some Dutch courage and then I jumped the barriers (as we all did) to bunk the fare. As I came out of the station and attempted to wade through the newspapers and assorted bits of rubbish that constantly flew about me, I suffered the disapproving stares of the car dealers on the Goldhawk Road. There they stood shivering on their lots, huddled together in their sheepskin coats, drinking black coffee and smoking incessantly as multi coloured bunting flapped about forlornly over their heads. 'Look at the fucking state of that,' they muttered as I trudged by.

As this was in the days before mobile phones were in the pocket of the common man, my visit was entirely on the off chance and when I arrived there, it was only to discover that in fact Pongo was back in Harrow keeping an appointment of his own with the local constabulary. However, he turned up again a bit later and was delighted to see me. I went on to mix great quantities of the dark, syrupy wine with chips and that resulted in some quite pleasantly coloured vomit later on. The whole crew were there and they set about entertaining me most royally. Tufty suddenly took his clothes off and we all threw things at him and Nig solicitously offered me aspirins when I was ill. He was being very quiet and organised and led Pinner and Pongo off with him on a reconnaissance to find a new squat. In the morning the sun came streaming brightly through the un-curtained windows and Pongo went off again with Nig and another scary bloke we knew as 'Drink wiv Me Dave', because they were due in court at ten.

Unfortunately, Zola did not fully share in my newfound joy and had actually said to me, 'I don't want you to get a boyfriend.' She had also had a couple of encounters with Tufty, whilst we were at the squat, so I felt it only fair to warn her that things could get dodgy there if Zazie got wind of it. These stresses brought about a scuffle one night in the shiny new bar of The Royal Beard, in which Zola ripped the diamante sparklers from my neck and Adam and some others held me back from committing violence ('only attack those smaller than yourself', says The Bully's Guide). A few days later, she sent me a twelve page letter detailing all my faults, but as I already knew them too well, I chucked it in the bin without ever bothering to read more than a couple of lines of it.

Pongo was a bit of a Mod at heart, he loved The Jam and he was also into Ska bands like Madness, The Specials and Bad Manners. I got into all that with him and we read the comics 'Viz' and '2,000 AD' and watched videos like 'Quadrophenia' and Alex Cox's film of 'Sid and Nancy.' Pongo was also keen on tales of London gang culture from the Sixties, perhaps because a member of his family had allegedly had some involvement with the notorious Richardson's. He had a T-shirt with an image of Ronnie and Reggie Kray on the front that said '*EastEnders*' and he wore fluorescent socks and royal blue suede 'Brothel Creeper' shoes. He was most keen on injecting speed and though I loved the drug, jacking or 'cranking' up, as Nig called it, was a past time that I never felt entirely comfortable with and had never practised myself. After a few months, I'd successfully put a stop to Pongo doing this for the rest of our time together (though I have a feeling that this may have had something to do with his weight increasing from thirteen stone to twenty).

On Friday March 6th 1987, after a gig of QOS's at the Hammersmith Greyhound, Pongo and I got the train to Shepherds Bush. We had a fab old time buying chips and walking through the deserted market, kicking through the detritus of the day and sending rubbish flying as we passed through the dimly lit thoroughfare. When we got to the squat, we found it empty because the others had moved out without telling him where they were going. Unconcerned by their absence, we settled in for the night and played our own games. Pongo always had LBC radio on no matter what and so we heard the news come in that the ferry The Herald of Free Enterprise had gone down at Zeebrugge 'with great loss of life.' I larked about in my lace-edged, pink silk camisole, my black fishnets and suspenders in that deserted, smashed up squat on a cold winter's night and I have to say that I was only half listening as countless poor souls breathed their last in the lonely, windswept reaches of the English Channel.

Grey dawn broke over the cold rooftops of North West London and Pongo and I began to pack up his stuff that the others had left behind. Then we went off to gather news of them. Firstly, we went to another block where a prostitute friend of theirs, Ann Marie, lived. She peered out of the door, at the top of a dingy flight of stairs. She had straggly hair and wore fluffy slippers and said she had no idea where the rest of his mates had gone (soon after this, she was found dead from a heroin overdose). We struggled along with his belongings in bulging carrier bags and went and had breakfast in a café round the corner. In there we met up with a mate of his who told us that the others had in fact decamped to a derelict pub in

Wandsworth. Pongo was not very pleased at this information, but this guy let him dump the stuff at his place whilst he sorted his life out and I went home to a normal house that had central heating.

A couple of days later, Leda and I went to meet Pongo at Ealing Common's District Line station. He looked a filthy sight sitting up on an electrical junction box and was smacked out of his head on Chinawhite. We went down to the old (and now practically derelict) Acorn Studios at Acton and scored some speed from the dealer who hung out at the place. We left Leda over there and the two of us went on down to 'Gossips', where we met up with all and sundry including Nig, who said that he'd never seen Pongo looking happier! Later we ended up at the Wandsworth brewery squat, a place that predictably absolutely stank of beer. It was an interesting building though and the interior was decorated with huge Victorian mirrors and dark, heavily carved woodwork that probably ended up either being totally destroyed by the developers or leaning against the damp wall of a reclamation yard. During our festivities, I accidentally poured some amyl down Pongo's nose, and what with that, chips, smack and quantities of snakebite and black, he was royally sick and pink pebble-dashed the outside wall. Zazie and Tufty had a big fight about Zola, so Zaz went to sleep with Nig. Then Pongo and I dossed on a mattress in Pinner's 'room'. I woke up in the night freezing to death and put the two bar electric fire on; it glowed dull orange in the gloom and the increasing heat made the beer fumes much stronger. In the morning Zaz went to the shops for us because we were all dying of dehydration and then Pinner, Pongo and I made our way back to Harrow.

On one of Pongo's little unexpected excursions in which

he was off the scene for ages, I headed for the pub and who should appear but Dolly's ex, a tall, well muscled and good looking bloke named Greg. We got into a long conversation about the old saga and our parts in it. He said that he wanted to kill Dolly (good idea) and Ian. The bottom line was that he was keen to get one over on Ian and I was eager to do the same to Dolly, but it was a shame that I didn't have more sense because for a while, things got into a bit of a muddle with him. He once turned up in the park when I was out with the dog and he had bought me loads of stuff. I can't say I didn't encourage him a tad, because it was great for the ego. Pongo was also quite friendly with him and one night we were all in the new improved (!) pub together and I thought, 'Oh dear'. Consequently, I took twelve Pro-Plus and six Do-Do's with tons of alcohol in order to blot it all out. Then Ian and Dolly arrived and you may not be all that surprised to find out that my stirring it up with poor Greg had brought it right to the fore in his mind again. So Greg went for Dolly, Ian stepped in to save her and Greg glassed him. As I came out of the pub I saw Ian standing there, pouring with blood from a cut under his eye, whilst stupid Dolly sat there crying. Sandra told me that Greg had mentioned to her that he was seeing one of Ian's exes and that Ian didn't like it. Ah, what an inaccurate statement that was! As if Ian gave a monkey's whom I saw. Anyway, a guy called Squiggy, who had a tattoo of a tear coming from his eye, took them up to the hospital and we all carried on again. Pongo was enjoying himself and wanted us to go back to QOS's new place, so we went, but I began to feel very wobbly indeed, what with the pills and the emotional excitement. I spent the whole night lying on her bed like a right party pooper and caffeine and I have not had a good relationship since that very day.

Things calmed down eventually and one evening Ian came over to speak to me at the pub. He expressed enormous surprise at the fact that Pongo and I were an item and he said, 'I'm really sorry that I've been such a bastard to you.'

A short time later, he turned up drunk on my doorstep late one night, when Pongo was there. I managed to get rid of him and then he phoned me, asked me out and made me promise to ring him back, but I never did because I just couldn't take any more of the particular type of 'stress' and 'hassle' that Ian gave me. It's sad really that I never did tell Ian how much I had loved him; because it was a bit late by the time I stood in the cemetery and watched as they lowered his coffin into the grave, on a wet April day in 1993.

So spring came, Pongo and I settled down together and the squat boys moved on without him, though we still visited them a lot. We went off to Saddlewhore's gigs and on another coach trip to The Riverside at Fetcham, where I slipped on some beer on the dance floor and broke my collar bone (I did not realise this 'til several months later) and we set light to some amyl at the back of the vehicle. We had started to follow another band called The Senseless Things, who were a talented little bunch of sixteen and seventeen year olds and they were the next generation now on their way up.

It was late in April and we were having one of those sudden hot spells, which as you may remember, from book one, have Londoners casting off their sweaters and laying about in parks. My not so skinny arms were burnt and Pongo and I were walking hand in hand up the Pinner Road towards the pub. A selection of ugly squared off cars with plastic bumpers went flashing by and even Pongo's mum's dark red Ford Sierra was now being converted to unleaded petrol. It had been a bit of a journey since I had dallied with gangly Miles in the sunny confines of Maida Vale and from him, I'd progressed to a drummer in make-up, dashing polo players, more drummers in make-up and now to a gauche lost boy with dried Evo-Stick upon his Parka. A middle-aged Irish couple came lurching towards us and they were also holding hands. They were drinking from cans of Tenants Super and the woman wore white stilettos on the end of mottled legs that dangled from the hem of her faded denim mini skirt. As they drew level with us the man winked, 'Isn't it grand to be in love?' He said.

'Yeah,' we answered in unison.

# THE END

# AFTERWORD

Surely you don't want to know what happened next? Because in order not to over-crowd the divorce courts I can't tell you! Only this. I got my teeth fixed against Pongo's wishes 'cos he knew I'd break his heart and I did. I still feel bad about that. I got married to a dish (now departed this life) and had the marvellous child. Later I found a fantastic partner, complete with Flambardy farm, who looked like Magnum PI, had been a millionaire MD at K-Tel Records (lost it in a divorce, hence later careers) and was straight out of a Jilly Cooper novel. He died of a brain haemorrhage on Boxing Day 2004, aged 51. The nod to him, is that he was one of the car dealers on the Goldhawk Road who often saw us punks walking by and shook his head in disbelief. Before he went I got my two English degrees BA/MA and fortunes see-sawed as usual a la Baker. Death lurks, the reaper is quite a pal, and many died. Good old CIN III also staged a comeback 23 years later.

As I mentioned, my beloved Lisa took her life. Ian had tried to contact me once or twice. He was run over by an articulated truck, in France, walking along the roadside at dusk. He was 27. Gaz was the one who phoned to tell me, because I guess he was the one who knew what it meant to me. Nig was hit by a train late in 2010. That was a blow, even though I hadn't seen much of him for years. I had always nurtured a fantasy that whenever I was at a boring straight occasion (it happened often with Magnum), there would be a knock on the door and Nig would appear with a bottle of vodka and say 'let's fuck off and get hammered'. So that was the end of that dream.

Nig's funeral was the last big gathering of the clan, but many of us are still close. In the pub afterwards, we all quite naturally broke off into our little sub groups of old. Pongo had become ultra cool, inherited the crown and taken charge of everything. We got drunk and I snogged two of the old gang, made friends with Sima and sat on Pongo's lap in the cab on the way home. Nig would have been so proud.

But I have to say I never got over Ian and he's my emotional repository for all loss, because I can never revisit him (as I have done with several of the others), and put it to rights. These were to me, my glory days and I know for sure that some of the gang feel the same. I do occasionally visit Ian's grave, neglected as it is now. Fortunately, whilst quietly communing with his bones, I've never yet bumped into Dolly!